HERTFORDSHIRE AND BEDFORDSHIRE

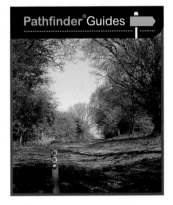

Outstanding
Circular Walks

Revised by
Louise Hall

Text: Brian Conduit, for the original text; Deborah King, for the
                    2008 and 2010 editions; and Louise Hall for the 2020 edition
Photography: Brian Conduit, Deborah King, except pp. 10 and 87
                    © Trotman Publishing and the Dean and Chapter of
                    St Albans Cathedral and pp. 69, 70 and 95
                    © Trotman Publishing and Woburn Abbey.
                    Front cover image iStock Photo © Alphotographic
Editorial: Ark Creative (UK) Ltd
Design: Ark Creative (UK) Ltd

ISBN 978-0-3190-9007-7

While every care has been taken to ensure the accuracy of the route directions, the
publishers cannot accept responsibility for errors or omissions, or for changes in
details given. The countryside is not static: hedges and fences can be removed, stiles
can be replaced by gates, field boundaries can be altered, footpaths can be rerouted
and changes in ownership can result in the closure or diversion of some
concessionary paths. Also, paths that are easy and pleasant for walking in fine
conditions may become slippery, muddy and difficult in wet weather, while stepping
stones across rivers and streams may become impassable.

If you find an inaccuracy in either the text or maps, please contact Trotman
Publishing at the address below.

First published 2003 by Jarrold Publishing.
Revised and reprinted 2008.

First published 2010 by Crimson Publishing. Reprinted with amendments in 2016,
2019 and 2020.

This edition first published 2021 by Trotman Publishing.

Trotman Publishing, 19-21D Charles Street, Bath, BA1 1HX
www.pathfinderwalks.co.uk

Printed in India by Replika Press Pvt. Ltd. 7/21

Front cover: Dunstable Downs, Bedfordshire
Previous page: Northchurch Common

Contents

The National Trust; The Ramblers; Walkers and the Law; Countryside Access Charter; Global Positioning System (GPS); Walking Safety; Useful Organisations; Ordnance Survey Maps

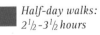 Short walks: up to 2¹/₂ hours

Half-day walks: 2¹/₂-3¹/₂ hours

 Longer walks: 3¹/₂-5 hours

Keymap

SCALE 1:312 500 or 1 INCH to 5 MILES *1CM to 3.1 KM*

KILOMETRES
0   2   4   6   8   10   15

MILES
0   2   4   6   8   10

SPOT HEIGHTS SHOWN IN METRES

ST NEOTS
Little Paxton
Great Paxton
Graveley
Papworth Everard
Elsworth
Lolworth
Impington
Milton
Girton
Hail Weston
Duloe
Staploe
Eaton Socon
Eynesbury
Toseland
Yelling
Knapwell
Bar Hill
Dry Drayton
Madingley
Chesterton
Wyboston
Croxton
Caxton Gibbet
Kingston
Great Eversden
Little Eversden
Haslingfield
Great Shelford
Roxton
Tempsford
Abbotsley
Longstowe
Little Gransden
Great Gransden
Waresley
Gamlingay
Hatley St George
Arrington
Wimpole Hall
Hauxton
Harston
Little Shelford
Blunham
Moggerhanger
Everton
Potton
Cockayne Hatley
East Hatley
Croydon
Wendy
Orwell
Whaddon
Shepreth
Foxton
Whittlesford
Northill
Ickwell
Sutton
Dunton
Wrestlingworth
Eyeworth
Tadlow
Shingay
Meldreth
Fowlmere
Thriplow
BIGGLESWADE
Southill
Broom
Edworth
Hinxworth
Abington Pigotts
Littlington
Bassingbourn
Kneesworth
Melbourn
Ickleton
Stanford
Langford
Ashwell
Steeple Morden
Guilden Morden
ROYSTON
Chrishall Grange
Shefford
Henlow
Clifton
Astwick
Caldecote
Newnham
Therfield
Barley
Newsells
Reed
Shaftenhoe End
Barkway
Flint Cross
Heydon
Great Chishill
Little Chishill
Duddenhoe End
Pond Green
Arlesey
Stottfold
Radwell
Bygrave
Kelshall
Sandon
Reed
Langley
Chrishall
Elmdon
Stotfold
Fairfield Park
Norton
Wallington
Buckland
Lower Green
Arkesden
LETCHWORTH GARDEN CITY
BALDOCK
Clothall
Redhill
Mill End
Chipping
Wyddial
Anstey
Meesden
Brent Pelham
Clavering
Ford End
HITCHIN
Ickleford
Weston
Rushden
Throcking
BUNTINGFORD
Great Hormead
Stocking Pelham
Berden
Holwell
Pirton
Willian
Great Wymondley
Hall's Green
Cromer
Cottered
Hare Street
Little Hormead
Hay Street
Furneux Pelham
East End
Manuden
Great Offley
Gosmore
Little Wymondley
Graveley
Great Ashby
Ardeley
Aspenden
Westmill
Braughing
Albury
Farnham
Ley Green
Preston
St Nicholas
WALKERN
Wood End
Braughing Friars
Albury End
Little Hadham
Breachwood Green
King's Walden
St Ippollitts
STEVENAGE
Aston End
Benington
Great Munden
Nasty
Puckeridge
A120
Hadham Ford
Bury Green
BISHOP'S STORTFORD
St Paul's Walden
Whitwell
Langley
Aston
Bragbury End
Hebing End
Haultwick
Colliers End
Standon
Wellpond Green
Much Hadham
Kimpton
Old Knebworth
KNEBWORTH
Datchworth
Dane End
Green End
Barwick
Latchford
Hadham Cross
Luton Airport
Peter's Green
Codicote
Woolmer Green
WATTON AT STONE
Sacombe
High Cross
Wadesmill
Bakers End
Blackmore End
Shaw's Corner
Oaklands
Bull's Green
Stapleford
Tonwell
Thundridge
Widford
New Mill End
Ayot St Lawrence
WELWYN
Digswell
Bramfield
Chapmore End
Wareside
Hunsdon
SAWBRIDGEWORTH
Lemsford
Ayot St Peter
Welwyn Garden City
Tewin Wood
Waterford
Birch Green
HERTFORD
WARE
Great Amwell
Hunsdonbury
High Wych
Matching Tye
Wheathampstead
Cromer Hyde
Stanborough
Cole Green
Hertingfordbury
St Margarets
Stanstead Abbotts
Gilston Park
HARLOW
Sandridge
Hatfield Garden Village
HATFIELD
Letty Green
Birch Green
Hertford Heath
Roydon
Broadley Common
ST ALBANS
Hatfield House
Woodside
Wildhill
Essendon
HODDESDON
Great Parndon
Hastingwood
Welham Green
Berkhamsted
Brickendon
Broxbourne
Lower Nazeing
Epping Green
Colney Heath
Bell Bar
Newgate Street
Wormley West End
Wormley
Nazeing
Thornwood Common
London Colney
Fragmore
Water End
Northaw
Hammond Street
Goffs Oak
Bumble's Green
EPPING
Colney Street
RADLETT
Shenleybury
Brookmans Park
South Mimms
Cuffley
CHESHUNT
WALTHAM ABBEY
Upshire
Fiddlers Hamlet
Aldenham
Shenley
Ridge
POTTERS BAR
Crews Hill
Waltham Cross
Hill Hall
Letchmore Heath
Wrotham Park
Botany Bay
Forty Hall
THEYDON BOIS
BOREHAMWOOD
Elstree
Monken Hadley
Enfield Chase
ENFIELD
High Beach
LOUGHTON
Abridge
Passingford Bridge
Bushey Heath
BARNET
Cockfosters
East Barnet
Ponders End
Winchmore Hill
Lambourne End
CHIGWELL
London Gateway
Totteridge
SOUTHGATE
CHINGFORD
Buckhurst Hill

At-a-glance...

Walk	Page	Start	Nat. Grid Reference	Distance	Height gain	Time
Ampthill Park and Millbrook Warren	72	Ampthill	TL 034382	8½ miles (13.7km)	735ft (225m)	4 hrs
Around Roxton	12	Roxton Village Hall	TL 152545	2½ miles (4.2km)	N/a	1½ hrs
Around Ashwell	26	Ashwell	TL 269397	5½ miles (8.6km)	280ft (85m)	2½ hrs
Ardeley, Benington and Walkern	60	Ardeley	TL 310272	7 miles (11.3km)	425ft (130m)	3½ hrs
Barkway, Reed and Earl's Wood	54	Barkway	TL 384356	6¼ miles (9.9km)	300ft (90m)	3 hrs
Bramfield Woods	16	Bramfield	TL 291156	4 miles (6.25km)	230ft (70m)	2 hrs
Bridgewater Monument and Aldbury	20	Bridgewater Monument	SP 971131	3½ miles (5.5km)	440ft (135m)	2 hrs
Chipperfield and Kings Langley	48	Chipperfield	TL 044015	6½ miles (10.5km)	480ft (145m)	3 hrs
Clophill, Wrest Park and Silsoe	78	Clophill	TL 082376	8¾ miles (14.1km)	545ft (165m)	4 hrs
Dunstable Downs and Totternhoe	38	Dunstable Downs Gateway Centre	TL 007195	5¼ miles (8.3km)	515ft (155m)	2½ hrs
Essendon and Little Berkhamsted	22	Essendon	TL 273087	4½ miles (7.2km)	505ft (155m)	2½ hrs
Hertford and the Cole Green Way	28	Hertford	TL 325125	5½ miles (8.6km)	410ft (125m)	2½ hrs
John Bunyan Country	64	Priory Country Park	TL 072493	7½ miles (12.1km)	145ft (45m)	3½ hrs
King's Wood and Houghton House	24	Houghton Conquest	TL 045415	4 miles (6.4km)	310ft (95m)	2 hrs
Northchurch Common and the Grand Union Canal	51	Berkhamsted	TL 991077	6 miles (9.7km)	395ft (120m)	3 hrs
Odell, Great Wood and Harrold	40	Harrold Odell Country Park	SP 956566	5¾ miles (9.2km)	260ft (80m)	2¾ hrs
Old Warden Park	18	Old Warden Park	TL 150448	4½ miles (7.2km)	245ft (75m)	2 hrs
Sandy and Everton	75	Sandy Market Square	TL 173492	9 miles (14.5km)	490ft (150m)	4 hrs
Sarratt and the River Chess	30	Chorleywood Common	TQ 032966	5¼ miles (8.4km)	440ft (135m)	2½ hrs
Sundon Hills and Sharpenhoe Clappers	43	Sundon Hills Country Park	TL 047285	5 miles (8.2km)	665ft (205m)	2½ hrs
Stockgrove Country Park	14	Stockgrove Country Park	SP 920293	3 miles (4.8km)	280ft (85m)	1½ hrs
St Albans and the Ver valley	86	St Albans	TL 147072	10½ miles (16.8km)	495ft (150m)	5 hrs
The Ayots, Brocket Park and the River Lea	82	Wheathampstead	TL 177140	10 miles (16.2km)	675ft (205m)	5 hrs
Turvey	36	Turvey Bridge	SP 936524	7 miles (11.1km)	360ft (110m)	3 hrs
Upper Lea valley and Someries Castle	57	Peter's Green	TL 142190	6½ miles (10.5km)	465ft (140m)	3 hrs
Ware, Stanstead Abbotts and Great Amwell	33	Ware	TL 356143	6¼ miles (10km)	165ft (50m)	3 hrs
Whitwell and St Paul's Walden	46	Whitwell	TL 184211	5¾ miles (9.1km)	425ft (130m)	2¾ hrs
Woburn Park and Eversholt	68	Woburn	SP 949331	7¼ miles (11.6km)	460ft (140m)	3½ hrs

Comments

There are fine views across Bedfordshire from the ridge walk through Ampthill Park and pleasant woodland walking in Millbrook Warren.

This easy but varied walk in the Ouse Valley follows attractive riverside paths and meadows and passes a quirky thatched chapel. It also offers a good opportunity to spot wildlife.

Ashwell is an attractive village and the tower and spire of its impressive church are in sight for much of the route.

Three picturesque villages are linked by this attractive walk in the valley of the Little River Beane in East Hertfordshire.

This figure-of-eight route links the villages of Barkway and Reed and includes much attractive woodland walking.

There are pleasant views and much enjoyable woodland walking on this route.

A combination of fine woodland, extensive views from the Chiltern escarpment and an exceptionally attractive village creates an absorbing and scenic walk.

The walk goes over commons, across fields and through woodland and there is a short stretch by the Grand Union Canal.

There are extensive views throughout and both historic and horticultural interest is provided by the ruined church at Clophill and the house and gardens at Wrest Park.

From the opening stretch along the curving rim of the Dunstable Downs, you enjoy superb and extensive views across the Vale of Aylesbury.

The route passes through two hilltop villages, and between them there is much fine woodland walking.

Much of the route is along the Cole Green Way, a former railway track, and there are fine views over the Lea valley.

The walk links Cardington, Elstow and Bedford and has a strong Bunyan theme. The finale is a beautiful stroll beside the Great Ouse at Bedford.

From Houghton Conquest, the route leads up through King's Wood to the ruins of Houghton House, a fine viewpoint.

An opening stretch through woodland and across open grassland is followed by a delightful return beside the Grand Union Canal.

The two attractive stone-built villages of Odell and Harrold are linked by pleasant field, lakeside and woodland paths.

This circuit around Old Warden Park starts by an exhibition of historic aircraft and includes views of a great house, attractive village and medieval church.

After walking along the base of the Greensand Ridge, you climb gently onto it to the village of Everton. From the ridge, the views are superb.

The highlights of the route are the pretty village of Sarratt, its isolated church and beautiful riverside walking beside the Chess.

A hilly walk by Bedfordshire standards, with superb views from both the ridge of the Sundon Hills and the beech-crowned summit of Sharpenhoe Clappers.

An easy and well-waymarked route, much of which is through attractive woodland.

Although lengthy, this is an undemanding walk which provides plenty of historic interest, as well as pleasant views over the valley of the River Ver.

Three villages, George Bernard Shaw's former home, a ruined church, views of a great house and beautiful walking through woods and by the River Lea, make up a fascinating route.

This pleasant and easy circuit of the countryside around the village of Turvey gives fine views over the valley of the Great Ouse.

An initial descent into the Lea valley is followed by a walk through it and a gentle climb, passing the remains of Someries Castle, back to the start.

Almost the whole of this flat and easy walk is beside water – either the River Lea or the parallel New River.

There are wide views and attractive woodland on this pleasant walk in Mimram valley, which passes the fine medieval church at St Paul's Walden.

Much of the route is across the open expanses of the deer park at Woburn and there are splendid views of the facade of Woburn Abbey.

Introduction to Hertfordshire and Bedfordshire

The common links between Hertfordshire and Bedfordshire – apart from the fact that they share a border – is that they rank among the smaller English counties, geologically they mainly comprise chalk and clay, and they have few hills. They are also counties that are difficult to categorise as they straddle more than one region. Bedfordshire sits between the East Midlands and East Anglia and belongs to both while Hertfordshire, although it may seem to be the archetypal Home County - particularly on its built-up and heavily suburbanised southern fringes - becomes more rural and flatter and takes on a distinctly East Anglian flavour the farther you get from London.

Both counties tend to be underrated by walkers, often overlooked in favour of the delights of the Thames Valley or the hillier Chiltern country of neighbouring Buckinghamshire. But they do possess much fine walking country, with a diversity of terrain, gentle hilly regions, lots of pleasant woodland, attractive riverside landscapes and an impressive collection of pretty villages.

Landscape and geography

Pleasant seems to be the most appropriate adjective to use when trying to sum up the landscape of Hertfordshire and Bedfordshire. In his *Buildings of England* series, Pevsner describes Bedfordshire as 'a county of pleasant, not of exciting landscape' and Hertfordshire's landscape as 'friendly, green, gently rolling, with no large river, uneventful but lovable'.

The nearest there is to an exciting landscape is looking westwards over the Vale of Aylesbury from the chalk escarpment of the Chilterns in west Hertfordshire and south-west Bedfordshire, or looking out from the greensand ridge that runs across mid-Bedfordshire. These views may appear rather tame when set against those found in the loftier and wilder northern and western regions of the country but they compare favourably with any found in other parts of southern and south-eastern England. It is precisely the lack of drama in their landscapes that is one of the most attractive scenic features of these counties. Everything is on a modest scale - gently undulating terrain, low hills, small areas of woodland and quiet rivers - revealing clearly that satisfying walking does not have to depend solely on the excitement of high peaks, wild moorland, great forests, mighty rivers or spectacular coastlines.

Hills and rivers

Although more closely identified with Buckinghamshire, the Chilterns run diagonally across part of west Hertfordshire and south-west Bedfordshire, before petering out north of Luton. From their western escarpment, there are a series of memorable views, especially from the wooded ridge at Ashridge and from the open, breezy heights of the Dunstable Downs. Small rivers like the Chess have cut attractive valleys through the hills and these have long been used as routeways between London and the rest of the country. This is well illustrated at Berkhamsted where the remains of a Norman castle overlook the valley of the little River Bulbourne, used by the Grand Union Canal, a trunk road (A41) and the main rail line between London and the Midlands, North West and Scotland.

One of the most outstanding physical features of the region is the greensand ridge which runs across the middle of Bedfordshire, roughly from Leighton Buzzard, on the Buckinghamshire border, to just beyond Sandy near the Cambridgeshire border. Greensand is a sandstone that contains a green iron-bearing mineral that gives the rock a greenish tint, seen in some churches and other buildings in the area. As sandy soils are poor in nutrients and therefore make poor agricultural land, much of the greensand ridge has never been cleared and remains well-wooded.

The major river in the region is the Great Ouse, which winds lazily across Bedfordshire, flowing through the heart of the county town. To the north of the Ouse valley is a belt of oolitic limestone and this has given rise to some of the most attractive villages in the area, not unlike their better-known Cotswold counterparts.

The only other river of any significance is the Lea, which rises in Bedfordshire and winds through the middle of Hertfordshire, also flowing

The trout lake, Roxton

St Albans Cathedral

through a county town. Other rivers – Ver, Chess, Bulbourne, Gade, Mimram, Rib and Beane – are little more than streams.

Places of historic interest

Neither county is particularly well-endowed with major historic attractions. There are no outstanding prehistoric monuments, little in the way of medieval abbeys and castles and, although there are many fine churches, they do not equal the great wool churches of the Cotswolds or those nearer at hand, just over the Essex border. The churches do have distinctive local characteristics. In Bedfordshire ironstone and sandstone predominates, except in the limestone north, while in Hertfordshire most churches are built of flint and often have 'spikes' instead of the usual spires above their towers.

A large proportion of the major historic sites are in and around St Albans, by far the most distinguished and interesting town in the region. It began life as Verulamium, one of the principal cities of Roman Britain. Most of the Roman city remains unexcavated but short stretches of its walls can be seen, plus foundations of one of the gateways and one of the finest Roman theatres in Britain. There is also a superb museum on the site. Medieval St Albans grew up on the other side of the Ver valley, around the abbey that was founded on the site of the martyrdom of Alban, Britain's first Christian martyr. The abbey was one of the largest and wealthiest in the country and in 1877 became the cathedral of a new diocese. It is the major ecclesiastical monument in the area.

The only medieval castle of any significance is at Berkhamsted and its remains are fairly scanty. Of the great castle that once controlled the crossing of the Great Ouse at Bedford, virtually nothing survives. What Hertfordshire and Bedfordshire lack in medieval buildings, they make up for in the quality and quantity of their great country houses. Finest of these is Woburn Abbey, seat of the dukes of Bedford, set amidst beautiful parkland that is fortunately accessible to walkers because of the network of public footpaths that cross it. Wrest Park, a huge Victorian mansion, and its formal gardens are nearby. Farther south in Hertfordshire are Hatfield House and Bishop's Palace, with their Elizabethan connections, and Knebworth House.

Literary connections

Both counties have strong literary associations. John Bunyan was born at Elstow near Bedford and wrote *The Pilgrim's Progress* while in Bedford jail.

A Bunyan Trail has been devised to link together the many places in the area associated with his life and work.

Hertfordshire's main literary connections are with George Bernard Shaw who lived at Ayot St Lawrence for the last 44 years of his life. His house, now maintained by the National Trust, remains much as he left it on his death in 1950.

Walking in the area

There are a large number of country parks, especially in Bedfordshire, which make excellent starting points for walks into the local countryside, linking up with the public footpath network. Both Hertfordshire and Bedfordshire have an extensive network of well-maintained rights-of-way and a large number of well-waymarked long-distance and recreational footpaths.

One of the finest is the Greensand Ridge Walk, which follows the well-wooded greensand ridge across Bedfordshire for 40 miles (64km). The Icknield Way Path heads across the region on its journey from the Chilterns to East Anglia. Two of these paths – the Ouse Valley Way and the Lea Valley Walk – have the two principal rivers as their theme, while the Grand Union Canal Walk keeps along the canal towpath. The Bunyan Trail has a literary theme while the Chiltern Way meanders through some of the hillier and most scenic areas of both counties.

Hopefully this introduction will whet the appetite for sampling an area which, with its wide views, mixture of wooded and open country, pleasant rivers and gently undulating terrain, provides attractive and satisfying walking, and all within easy reach of the heavily populated areas of London and the Home Counties.

This book includes a list of waypoints alongside the description of the walk, so that you can enjoy the full benefits of gps should you wish to. For more information about route navigation, improving your map reading ability, walking with a GPS and for an introduction to basic map and compass techniques, read Pathfinder® Guide *Navigation Skills for Walkers* by outdoor writer Terry Marsh (ISBN 978-0-319-09175-3). This title is available in bookshops and online at os.uk/shop

Around Roxton

Start	Roxton Village Hall	GPS waypoints
Distance	2½ miles (4.2km)	TL 152 545
Height gain	Negligible	Ⓐ TL 153 545
Approximate time	1½ hours	Ⓑ TL 159 540
Parking	In the High Street near the village hall	Ⓒ TL 159 534
		Ⓓ TL 152 535
Ordnance Survey maps	Explorer 208 (Bedford & St Neots), Landranger 153 (Bedford & Huntingdon)	

This short and easy walk explores the meadows and riverside paths of the River Great Ouse and the village of Roxton. Although sandwiched between the A421 and the A1, this attractive route is surprisingly quiet and unspoilt and a haven for wildlife.

Begin at the village hall in the High Street and, with your back to it, turn right and head towards the nearby **Royal Oak** pub at the crossroads. Turn right (School Lane) and at the church of St Mary turn right, at a public footpath sign to Roxton Lock, and go over a stile Ⓐ.

The church dates from the 14th century, has a tower that was added in the 15th century, and inside a screen dado depicting Saints. Follow the path keeping to the left of the church and head diagonally through the churchyard towards a large weeping willow tree in the corner. At a public footpath sign pass a barrier and continue along an attractive enclosed

Congregational church, Roxton

path that separates two fields and passes to the left of a pond. At a T-junction turn left at a waymarked post and follow the path, with a hedge on one side and a young tree plantation on the other.

Follow the path round first a left and then a right bend and keep ahead at a path junction and waymarked post to continue downhill through a small copse and then cross a footbridge and go over a stile to enter a field. Continue ahead, along the left edge of a field and at the field corner, go over another stile. Keep ahead along this curving riverside path, past a footbridge on the left, to reach a public footpath sign to Roxton Lock **B**.

Go over a footbridge and a stile to enter a meadow. Turn left and continue along the grassy path and at the next waymarked post bear right along an attractive stretch of the River Great Ouse. Cross a footbridge and follow the meandering path that runs to the left of a wire fence. At a waymarked post keep ahead and climb a stile.

Follow the path across a bridge over the old Roxton Lock. Go across another footbridge and the path bends sharp right beside a wooden fence. To your left is the modern lock built in 1972. Do not cross the footbridge over the river here but pass to the right of the NRA building and then a barrier waymarked Ouse Valley Way **C**.

Continue along a narrow enclosed path to the right of the river. Where the trees end you will see a large trout lake on the right. This section of the walk is a good place to see and hear wildlife including heron, kingfisher, coot, great

crested grebe and mallard.

The path later becomes enclosed before emerging onto a wide, grassy path at the fence corner **D**.

Turn right to head away from the river and follow this path across a tarmac track before heading gently uphill to the village. Where the path forks at a waymarked sign bear right along a narrow, enclosed path to reach a lane.

Turn right and at a road junction, at a small triangular green, turn left into the High Street. Follow the lane and shortly, on the left, you will pass the unusual congregational church, one of only two thatched chapels in England. It was once a barn and converted into a place of worship in 1808 by a local squire, Charles Metcalfe. It has ogee-pointed, or concave and convex, curved windows and a verandah made of twisted tree trunks. Services are held here on Sunday evening.

Continue ahead to return to the start of the walk. ●

Stockgrove Country Park

		GPS waypoints
Start	Stockgrove Country Park, on minor road to Great Brickhill to the north-east of Reach and Heath	 SP 920 293 Ⓐ SP 920 283 Ⓑ SP 908 287 Ⓒ SP 915 298 Ⓓ SP 919 300
Distance	3 miles (4.8km)	
Height gain	280 feet (85m)	
Approximate time	1½ hours	
Parking	Stockgrove Country Park	
Ordnance Survey maps	Explorer 192 (Buckingham & Milton Keynes), Landranger 165 (Aylesbury & Leighton Buzzard)	

Most of the walk is either through or along the edge of the beautiful woodlands that make up Stockgrove Country Park, part of a former estate. The route is easy, well-waymarked and from various points on the edge of the trees, there are pleasant views over gently rolling country on the Bedfordshire – Buckinghamshire border.

Begin by turning right out of the car park and almost immediately turn right again, at a public footpath sign, through a kissing-gate. At a fork, take the left-hand path, waymarked Circular Route, through Baker's Wood. This is an oak wood and, together with nearby King's Wood, makes up the largest remaining area of deciduous woodland in Bedfordshire.

After going through a kissing-gate, keep ahead along a fence-lined path and continue to a T-junction by Heath and Reach British Legion Club Ⓐ. Turn right and at a fork take the left-hand path – there is a Circular Route post ahead – through a delightful area of trees, gorse and glades to a kissing-gate. Go through and continue gently uphill over a brow and then descend steeply to cross a footbridge over a brook. Head uphill through conifers, cross a track at the top, keep ahead and the path descends to a T-junction and footpath post on the edge of the trees Ⓑ.

Turn right – here joining the Greensand Ridge Walk – onto a path that keeps along the left inside edge of Oak Wood. Go through a kissing-gate, keep to the left of a pond, head uphill to a crossways, turn right and continue uphill. Keep ahead at the next

Baker's Wood

Stockgrove Country Park

crossways and the track emerges from the trees and passes to the left of Stockgrove House, built in the 1920s on the site of an earlier one. Continue to a lane **C** and bear right. Where the lane curves right, turn left, at a public bridleway sign, along an enclosed path by the left edge of woodland.

At a public footpath sign to Stockgrove Country Park, turn right over a stile **D**, cross a track, bear right, pass beside a fence, at a Circular Route waymark, and continue through woodland to a kissing-gate on the far side. Go through and follow the grassy path ahead through a gently sloping valley fringed by trees. The path leads to a kissing-gate onto a lane opposite the start. ●

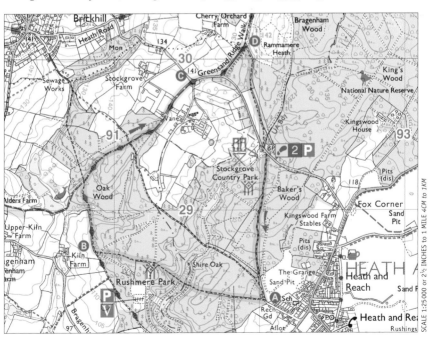

Bramfield Woods

Start	Bramfield	GPS waypoints
Distance	4 miles (6.25km)	✐ TL 291 156
Height gain	230 feet (70m)	Ⓐ TL 291 159
Approximate time	2 hours	Ⓑ TL 282 170
Parking	Bramfield, lay-by with parking spaces along Main Road near village centre	Ⓒ TL 278 161
		Ⓓ TL 288 147
Ordnance Survey maps	Explorer 182 (St Albans & Hatfield), Landranger 166 (Luton & Hertford)	

A good proportion of the walk is through the delightful woodlands that lie to the north and west of the village of Bramfield. Two forays into more open country reveal extensive views over the surrounding terrain. Expect muddy conditions at times on some of the woodland tracks and paths.

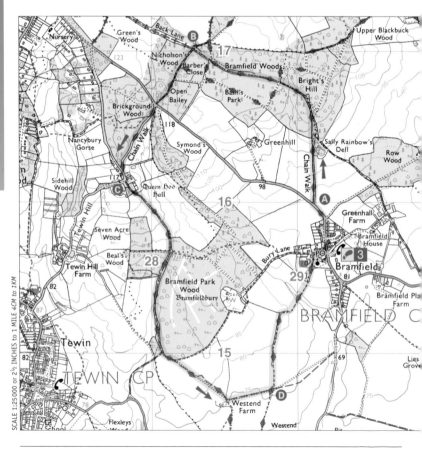

SCALE 1:25000 or 2½ INCHES to 1 MILE 4CM to 1KM

Thatched cottage at Bramfield

The quiet and secluded village of Bramfield has the **Queens Head** pub, a picturesque thatched post office – once the village school – and a medieval church. The latter was so extensively restored in 1840 that it has a decidedly Victorian appearance.

Start in the village centre at the junction of Main Road and Bury Lane and, facing the Village Well House, turn left along Main Road. Follow it out of the village, curving left, and at a public bridleway sign to Datchworth Green, turn right along a tree-lined path **A**. After passing a waymarked post, the path continues through woodland, curving gradually left. Keep ahead at the first two crossways, following public bridleway signs, but at the third one where there is a fingerpost, turn left along the bridleway signposted to Symonds Wood **B**. The path emerges onto a lane at a junction.

Take the narrow lane opposite (Tewin Hill), between Brickground Wood on the right and Symonds Wood on the left, keep ahead at a junction and where the

lane bends right, turn left **C**, at a public bridleway sign to Tewin, along an enclosed track. The track continues gently downhill across a field before entering Bramfield Park Wood. Take the broad track through the wood and at a fork on the edge of the trees, continue along the left-hand track by the right inside edge of the wood. Curve left to join another track and on emerging from the trees, keep ahead at first along the left edge of a field, and then follow the track across fields to a path junction by an area of scrub and trees.

At a waymark post, turn left along a straight track and at a crossways by a footpath post, turn left again **D** along a path that mostly keeps along a low embankment between fields. The path curves right to keep by the left field edge and where the hedge on the left ends, continue gently downhill across the field to cross a ditch.

Head gently uphill across the next field to a footpath post and pass through a fence gap. Now continue across a sports field, then go through a gate by the side of the village hall and onto a road before turning right to the start.

Old Warden Park

		GPS waypoints
Start	Old Warden Park, Shuttleworth Collection entrance	TL 150 448
Distance	4½ miles (7.2km)	Ⓐ TL 154 448
Height gain	245 feet (75m)	Ⓑ TL 157 441
		Ⓒ TL 148 430
Approximate time	2 hours	Ⓓ TL 138 440
Parking	Old Warden Park	Ⓔ TL 137 447
Ordnance Survey maps	Explorer 208 (Bedford & St Neots), Landranger 153 (Bedford & Huntingdon)	

This lovely ramble is basically a circuit of Old Warden Park, taking in Old Warden village and church. There are fine views across the park, pleasant wooded stretches and the opportunity to sample the many and varied attractions of the park which include a collection of historic aircraft, birds of prey, a great Victorian house and an early 19th-century Swiss Garden.

Old Warden Park was bought by the Shuttleworth family in 1872 and houses the Shuttleworth Collection of historic aeroplanes and vehicles, the Swiss Garden (a romantic landscape garden), a falconry centre and Shuttleworth College. This ornate Victorian mansion, former home of the Shuttleworths, is now used for conferences, courses and wedding and other receptions.

Start by turning right along the road and after ¼ mile (400m), turn right Ⓐ, at a public bridleway sign, and walk along a path which keeps by the meandering right edge of a field. Look out for where a public bridleway sign directs you to turn right and cross a footbridge over a brook. Continue on the path, keeping the brook on the right and then walk along the right edge of fields. Pass small ponds on your right, reaching a gate. Go through, keeping ahead by the left edge of the field, go through a second gate and turn right along a tarmac drive.

At a Circular Route sign, to the right

of the wood turn left through a redundant gate Ⓑ and bear right along the right edge of a field. Follow the edge as it curves left and on the far side, go through a wide gap and walk initially along the right edge of the next field. Reaching the end the trees (right – Lowsiebush Cover), cross a road and continue along the right edge of the

Old Warden church

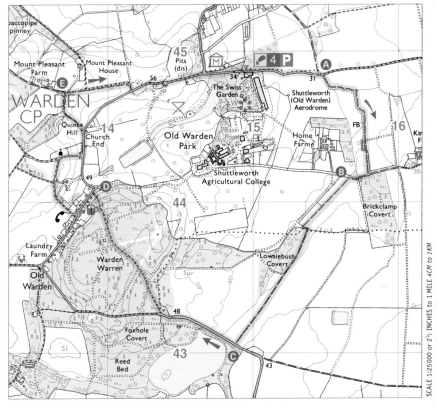

next field to emerge onto a lane **C**. Turn right and on entering woodland ahead, turn right through a kissing-gate, at a public footpath sign, and continue along a track through the mainly conifer woodland of Warden Warren.

At a fork, take the left-hand fence-lined track, and keep ahead along a path which descends steps and passes through four barriers onto a road in Old Warden **D**. Turn left through this estate village, largely redesigned in a Swiss style in the early 19th century and contemporary with the Swiss Garden. Just beyond the **Hare and Hounds** pub, turn right, at a public footpath sign, along an enclosed path which continues gently uphill along the right edge of a field. Climb steps in the corner and keep along the right edge of the next two fields, and through two kissing-gates, to emerge onto a lane in front of Old

Warden church. This dates from the 12th century and retains some Norman features.

Turn right and as you head downhill, there are superb views ahead of the park, lake and Shuttleworth College. At a T-junction, turn left and where the road bends right, bear left, at a public bridle-way sign, along the concrete drive to Mount Pleasant Farm and Shuttleworth College Equine Centre. The drive curves right and in front of the entrance to the farm, turn right through a gate **E**.

Keep ahead along a track across a field and just before reaching a track on the far side, turn right, passing down the left side of a field to go through a gap to rejoin the road. Turn left, keep ahead at a junction and the road leads back to the start. ●

Bridgewater Monument and Aldbury

Bridgewater Monument and Aldbury

		GPS waypoints
Start	Bridgewater Monument, off B4506 between Northchurch and Dagnal	
Distance	3½ miles (5.5km)	
Height gain	440 feet (135m)	
Approximate time	2 hours	
Parking	Bridgewater Monument	
Ordnance Survey maps	Explorer 181 (Chiltern Hills North), Landranger 165 (Aylesbury & Leighton Buzzard)	

GPS waypoints

- 🖉 SP 971 131
- Ⓐ SP 970 133
- Ⓑ SP 963 136
- Ⓒ SP 953 129
- Ⓓ SP 962 124

The walk starts on the Chiltern escarpment amidst the delightful woodlands of the Ashridge Estate. From here it descends and continues by a golf course and across fields to the picturesque village of Aldbury, nestling below the escarpment. A fairly steep but short climb through woodland leads back to the start.

The Bridgewater Monument was erected in 1832 in memory of the third Duke of Bridgewater, the great canal builder and owner of Ashridge. The view from the top is well worth the climb.

🖉 Start in front of the Ashridge Estate Visitor Centre, walk across the grass to the monument and just beyond it, cross a track and keep ahead through woodland, following Ashridge Estate Boundary Trail signs. After about 200 yards, look out for a yellow-waymarked post on the left Ⓐ and bear left along a path which heads gently downhill. Pass beside a barrier and continue down across the thickly wooded face of the escarpment along a track which curves left and emerges from the trees.

The track passes to the left of a farm, continues to a gate and onto a lane Ⓑ. Go through a fence gap opposite, walk along the right inside edge of Walk Wood and then continue along the right edge of Stocks golf course. The path

later keeps by the left edge of woodland, continuing along the curving edge of the course. After curving right by a fingerpost, follow it around a left bend and at a fingerpost by the next right bend, turn left Ⓒ over a stile and take a path that heads in a straight line across the golf course, the route indicated by a succession of posts. Climb a stile on the far side, go through the kissing-gate opposite and continue along an enclosed path towards Aldbury Church. Go through a kissing-gate, keep ahead to go through another one and walk along an enclosed path. Go through another kissing-gate and keep along the right edge of a field by farm buildings on the right. Go through a kissing-gate, continue across a field, go through a kissing-gate onto a road Ⓓ and turn left into Aldbury, passing the church and continuing to the crossroads in the village centre.

All the ingredients that make up the classic English village scene are present

the green; and a short distance away there is a medieval church. To enhance the scene still further, the village is set against the glorious backdrop of the beech woods of Ashridge. It is not surprising that Aldbury has frequently been used as a film set.

At the crossroads, keep ahead along Toms Hill Road and at a public bridleway sign, bear left along an enclosed track, signposted to Monument, **Tea Room** and Shop. The track heads uphill through woodland, later ascending more steeply and with steps in places. Bear left on meeting another path and continue up, following

Bridgewater Monument

in Aldbury: charming brick and half-timbered cottages (some thatched) and a pub, the **Greyhound Inn**, grouped around a triangular green; duck pond, stocks and whipping-post standing on

Ashridge Estate Boundary Trail signs, back to the start. ●

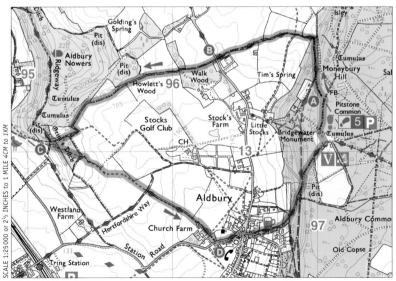

Essendon and Little Berkhamsted

		GPS waypoints
Start	Essendon	 TL 273 087
Distance	4½ miles (7.2km)	Ⓐ TL 272 088
Height gain	505 feet (155m)	Ⓑ TL 266 082
Approximate time	2½ hours	Ⓒ TL 276 072
Parking	Roadside parking – not on the main road – at Essendon	Ⓓ TL 291 079
		Ⓔ TL 273 087
Ordnance Survey maps	Explorer 182 (St Albans & Hatfield), Landranger 166 (Luton & Hertford)	

Considering the proximity of the M25 and the northern fringes of London, this is a remarkably unspoilt and tranquil route with a genuinely remote feel. Both Essendon and Little Berkhamsted are hilltop villages and command fine views over the surrounding countryside. Much of this terrain is well-wooded and there are some delightful woodland stretches, as well as field paths and quiet lanes.

Start by Essendon's 19th-century church and walk along the lane, passing to the right of it. At a public footpath sign No.17, turn left Ⓐ along a narrow, enclosed path and climb a stile. Walk diagonally across a field, go through a kissing-gate in the corner and keep ahead to go through another one.

Walk along the left edge of a field, go through a kissing-gate, bear right across the next field and go through another kissing-gate to a T-junction. Turn right to keep along the right inside edge of woodland, continue downhill through the wood (Backhouse Wood) and on emerging from the trees, cross a footbridge over Essendon Brook. Keep ahead, go through a kissing-gate, continue along the right edge of a field and go through another kissing-gate to a T-junction Ⓑ.

Turn left, head gently uphill along an attractive, tree-lined track and after

¼ mile (400m), bear left, at a footpath post, and go through a kissing-gate. Keep ahead through trees and continue along the left edge of a field. At the corner, bear left along a faint path – do

---

Little Berkhamsted war memorial

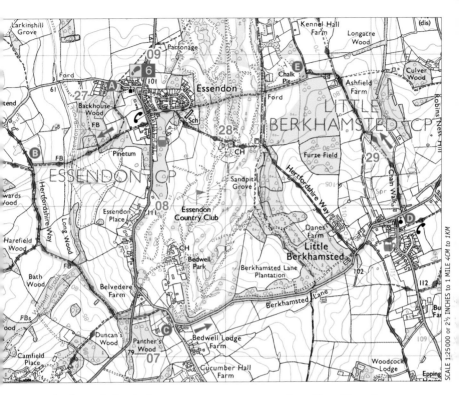

not take the track ahead – into woodland and just beyond a waymarked post, cross a plank footbridge over a brook. The next part of the route is through this delightful woodland. At a crossways by a fingerpost, keep ahead and at the next footpath post, the path bends left. Descend steps, cross a footbridge over a brook, ascend steps and walk on to climb more steps onto a road.

Cross over and head gently uphill along an enclosed path, curving right to emerge onto a lane at a junction **C**. Keep ahead along Berkhamsted Lane for 1¼ miles (2km) into the pleasant village of Little Berkhamsted and just beyond the mainly Victorian church and the war memorial, turn left **D** along a tarmac track (Breach Lane). After ¼ mile (400m) – just after the lane bears slightly left – turn left through a gate and head gently downhill to the right of a fence. In the far corner, keep

ahead over a footbridge and walk along an enclosed path – this is narrow and may be overgrown – to emerge onto a tarmac track.

Keep ahead and where the track bends right, go over a stile and turn left along a path **E**. Ignore the path ahead and go over another stile on the right. Walk along a path by a fence on the right which borders a chalk pit, and climb another stile.

Turn right to a crossways and keep ahead to join a tarmac track. Follow it uphill across a golf course and on the far side, pass beside a barrier and keep ahead – first along an enclosed path and then along a road – to a T-junction in Essendon. Turn left for the **Rose and Crown**, or to complete the walk, turn right, and then at the war memorial bear left along Church Street. ●

King's Wood and Houghton House

Start	Houghton Conquest	**GPS waypoints**	
Distance	4 miles (6.4km)		TL 045 415
Height gain	310 feet (95m)	A	TL 044 412
Approximate time	2 hours	B	TL 045 405
Parking	Roadside parking at Houghton Conquest	C	TL 039 392
		D	TL 038 401
Ordnance Survey maps	Explorers 208 (Bedford & St Neots) and 193 (Luton & Stevenage), Landranger 153 (Bedford & Huntingdon)		

An easy climb through King's Wood leads onto the Greensand Ridge, from which there are extensive views over mid-Bedfordshire. The walk continues past the atmospheric ruins of Houghton House, which occupy a commanding position on the ridge, before descending across fields and along the edge of the wood to return to the start. Some of the paths and tracks may be muddy after wet weather.

In the imposing, battlemented, mainly 15th-century church at Houghton Conquest there are tombs of the Conquest family from which the village gets its name.

Start in High Street and, facing the post office, turn left towards the church. Reaching Rectory Lane A, turn left along it and at a public footpath sign, turn left along an enclosed path. On entering a field, turn right along its right edge, follow the edge around right and left bends and before reaching the corner, look out for where you turn right through a kissing-gate.

Turn left to continue along the left edge of the next field, go through a kissing-gate and turn right along the right inside edge of woodland. In front of a kissing-gate, turn left B, head uphill through King's Wood, a block of ancient woodland, keeping by a wire fence on the right, and go through a kissing-gate

The ruins of Houghton House

on the brow. Continue along the left edge of the trees, following the curving edge to where waymarks direct you to go through the kissing-gate ahead (not the gate into the wood). Walk along the left edge of a field and keep ahead along an enclosed track. From this position on the greensand ridge, there are fine and extensive views to the right across mid-Bedfordshire. After passing to the left of barns, the track bends right to a T-junction and ahead are the ruins of Houghton House 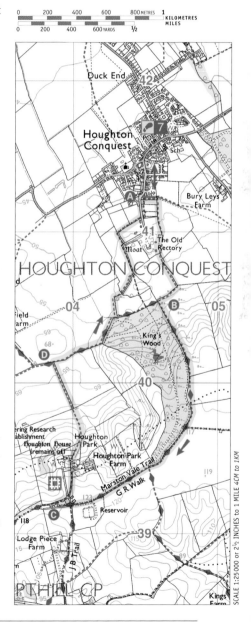. This impressive mansion, originally built by the Countess of Pembroke in the early 17th century as a hunting lodge, was later abandoned and fell into ruin. It occupies a fine position on the ridge and is thought to be 'The House Beautiful' in John Bunyan's, *The Pilgrim's Progress.*

At the T-junction, turn right along a concrete track which curves left and where it bends right to Houghton Park Farm, keep ahead towards the house. Before reaching a gate, bear right and head down across grass to a waymarked stile. Climb it, continue gently downhill along the left edge of a field and at a fence corner, keep ahead to a gate. Go through, continue gently downhill across a sloping field – Houghton Conquest Church can be seen ahead – cross a footbridge on the far side and keep straight on along the right edge of the next field.

Cross another footbridge in the corner and turn right D along the right edge of a field towards King's Wood again. After crossing a small stream, head gently uphill along the right edge of the next field and follow it as it curves left alongside the wood. Turn right along the right edge of a field and in the corner, turn left to continue along the right edge, following it to the right. In the next corner, keep ahead through trees, go through a kissing-gate, walk along

an enclosed path and go through a gate to a T-junction.

Turn left along an enclosed track and where it bends right to a gate, keep ahead through a kissing-gate and continue along a fence-lined path. Follow it round to the right and cross a stream to emerge onto a lane. Turn left back to Houghton Conquest. ●

Around Ashwell

		GPS waypoints
Start	Ashwell	🥾 TL 269 397
Distance	5½ miles (8.6km)	Ⓐ TL 269 403
Height gain	280 feet (85m)	Ⓑ TL 258 408
Approximate time	2½ hours	Ⓒ TL 255 401
Parking	Roadside parking at Ashwell	Ⓓ TL 262 392
Ordnance Survey maps	Explorers 193 (Luton & Stevenage) and 208 (Bedford & St Neots), Landranger 153 (Bedford & Huntingdon)	Ⓔ TL 266 380
		Ⓕ TL 274 382

A combination of quiet lanes and field paths makes up a pleasant circuit of the gently undulating country to the north, west and south of the attractive village of Ashwell. Wide expanses and extensive views give the walk a decidedly East Anglian feel, not perhaps surprising as it is close to the Hertfordshire – Cambridgeshire border.

The number of impressive buildings along the High Street at Ashwell, many of them timber-framed and dating from between the 15th and 17th centuries, and in particular the handsome church, are evidence of its former prosperity as an important market centre. The church is unusually large and imposing for a village church. It was built in the 14th century and the tower and spire, over 170 feet (52m) high, are in sight for much of the route.

🥾 Start in High Street by the post office and the **Three Tuns** and, facing the pub, turn left. Turn right along Church Lane, turn left into Swan Street and turn right along Mill Street, passing to the left of the church. Just after crossing the little River Rhee and where the lane bends right, keep ahead through a kissing-gate and walk along the left edge of a field. Go through another kissing-gate onto a lane Ⓐ, turn left and take the first lane on the left.

At a public footpath sign, turn right over a stile, walk across a field to the corner of woodland and continue along the right edge of the trees. At the corner

Ashwell

of the wood, keep ahead across the field, veering slightly right to climb a stile, keep in the same direction across the next field, making for the left corner of trees, and climb a stile onto a lane **B**.

Turn left, follow the lane around as it bends first left, then right, to continue ahead at the T-junction. The path bends left and where it bends right again, keep ahead **C**, at a public byway sign, along an attractive, hedge– and tree-lined path to a road.

Turn left, at a T-junction turn right and almost immediately turn left **D**, at a public byway sign, along a hedge-lined track (Partridge Hill). The track first heads steadily uphill over the low ridge to the south of Ashwell and then descends gently along the left edge of a field. At the bottom, turn left along the right edge of a field to a road **E**, turn left and at a public footpath sign, turn right onto a path.

The path heads in a straight line across fields to a lane **F**. Turn left and head over the low ridge again, descending into Ashwell. The lane leads directly back to High Street near the starting point. ●

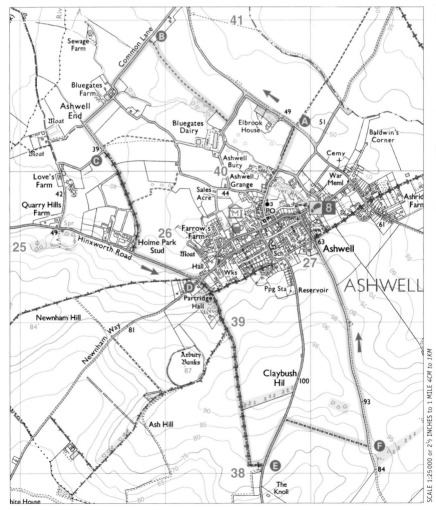

Hertford and the Cole Green Way

		GPS waypoints
Start	Hertford, Parliament Square	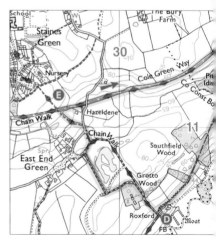 TL 325 125
Distance	5½ miles (8.6km)	Ⓐ TL 323 122
Height gain	410 feet (125m)	Ⓑ TL 320 121
Approximate time	2½ hours	Ⓒ TL 309 116
Parking	Hertford	Ⓓ TL 302 104
Ordnance Survey maps	Explorers 194 (Hertford & Bishop's Stortford) and 182 (St Albans & Hatfield), Landranger 166 (Luton & Hertford)	Ⓔ TL 295 111

The first and last parts of this undemanding walk are through the castle grounds at Hertford and along a most attractive, tree-lined, former railway track. In between there are fine, open views over the Lea valley.

Attractive old buildings line the narrow streets and small squares in the town centre of Hertford. Of its once great medieval castle, little is left apart from the mound, some of the outer walls and the 15th-century, brick-built gatehouse, modernised and extended around 1800.

Start by the war memorial in Parliament Square, turn right towards the river and turn left into the castle grounds. At a fork, take the right-hand tarmac path to keep briefly beside the River Lea, turn left in front of the restored gatehouse of Hertford Castle, turn left again and almost immediately turn right to pass to the right of the castle walls. Turn left and then right to a road, by a Lea Valley Walk sign, cross it and descend steps to pass under a subway. Turn right up a slope, keep ahead along a path beside the dual carriageway and turn left down the slope into West Street.

After passing in front of the **Black Horse** pub, turn left Ⓐ along an enclosed path, follow it around a right bend, keep ahead and descend steps to a road. Turn right and then almost immediately turn sharp left Ⓑ, at a Cole Green Way sign, along a tarmac track and cross a bridge over the river. Continue along the broad track and pass beside a gate to join the Cole Green Way, the former railway line between

Hertford and Welwyn Junction, now converted into a footpath and bridleway.

Walk along a fence-lined track, pass under a railway viaduct, continue through woodland, turn right to pass beside a gate and then turn left. Keep along this attractive, tree-lined track as far as a blue-waymarked post where you bear left **C** down steps to a lane. Bear left and where the lane curves left, turn right, at a public bridleway sign, pass beside a barrier and walk along an enclosed track, by the left edge of woodland. After passing the corner of the wood, the track keeps ahead – along the left edge of fields and through woodland – eventually bending first left and then right to reach a gate by a fingerpost.

Go through the kissing-gate on the right **D** and head gently uphill along an enclosed track, signposted to East End Green. Bear right, pass beside a

gate and bear left to continue between a fence on the right and woodland on the left and at a fork bear left along a wide grassy path beside the wood. Turn right to cross a quarry track and go through a kissing-gate. At the end of the enclosed path turn right at a fingerpost to a lane. Turn right and at a public footpath sign, turn left over a stile and walk along the right edge of two fields, climbing a stile separating them.

Go through a kissing-gate and cross a plank footbridge, go up steps and turn right to rejoin the Cole Green Way **E**. Cross a lane, descend steps, bear left and follow the track back to Hertford. After crossing a bridge over a lane **C**, you rejoin the outward route and retrace your steps to the start. ●

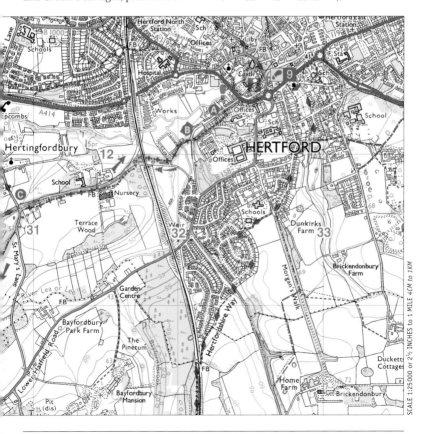

Sarratt and the River Chess

		GPS waypoints	
Start	Chorleywood Common, off A404	TQ 032 966	
Distance	5¼ miles (8.4km)	Ⓐ TQ 034 967	
Height gain	440 feet (135m)	Ⓑ TQ 039 973	
Approximate time	2½ hours	Ⓒ TQ 031 983	
Parking	Car park at Chorleywood Common	Ⓓ TQ 032 988	
Ordnance Survey maps	Explorer 172 (Chiltern Hills East),	Ⓔ TQ 040 996	
	Landranger 176 (West London)	Ⓕ TQ 042 993	
		Ⓖ TQ 038 983	

There are fine views and much attractive riverside walking through the Chess valley on this route on the eastern fringes of the Chilterns. Sarratt is an exceptionally pretty village and the walk passes its mainly Norman church at Church End, nearly one mile (1.6km) from the village centre.

There are a couple of car parks south of the A404 along the northern fringe of Chorleywood Common: from the westernmost one, turn right out of it and walk towards the second parking area almost opposite the tarmac drive Ⓐ of Chorleywood House Estate. Go left up the drive and where it bends left, turn right along a track and at a fork, take the left-hand, tree-lined track which heads gently downhill.

At the next path junction, continue ahead, signposted Valley Walk, along a path which winds more steeply downhill through woodland and at a footpath post just before reaching a tarmac track, turn left along a tree-lined path Ⓑ. After going through a gate and emerging from the trees, keep ahead along a path beside the River Chess,

River Chess

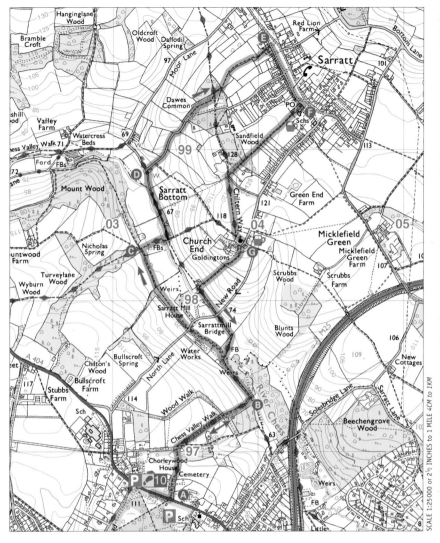

later bearing left away from the river to a tarmac track by the gates of Chorleywood Pumping Station. Turn right along the track to a lane, cross over, go through a kissing-gate at a public footpath sign to Chenies, and walk along the left edge of a field.

Go through a kissing-gate, keep ahead by a fence on the right, to pass through another kissing-gate to continue on the hedge-lined path. At the crossways, before a gate leading into woodland, turn right **C**, in the Sarratt church direction. Cross a

footbridge, keep ahead to cross another over the River Chess and at a public footpath signposted Chess Valley Walk, turn left through a kissing-gate. Walk along an enclosed path – it later becomes a tarmac track – and at the corner of a lane, turn right uphill **D**. Just after the lane enters woodland, bear left, at a public footpath sign to Sarratt Green, along a path to a footpath post. Bear left and the path curves right

Sarratt church

up through the trees to a fork.

Take the left-hand path to a T-junction, turn right to a junction of paths, turn left and go through a kissing-gate on the edge of the woodland. Walk across a field to a fence corner and continue along the right field edge to a kissing-gate. Pass through, keep ahead along a tree-lined track to a road **E** and turn right into Sarratt, an outstandingly attractive village with houses, cottages and inns -**The Cricketers** and **The Cock** - lining its wide and spacious green. Just before the two roads which run along both sides of the green meet, turn right, at a public footpath sign to Church End **F**, along an enclosed tarmac track to a kissing-gate.

Go through and the route continues along the left edge of the next three fields, using two gates. After going through a kissing-gate in the corner of the third field, head gently downhill, along an enclosed path, through woodland to a tarmac track. Cross it and bear left to go through a kissing-gate, and immediately through another gate, walk along the top edge of a sloping field and at a fence corner, keep ahead across the field towards Sarratt church. On the far side of the field go through a kissing-gate, walk ahead and take the kissing-gate into the churchyard. Pass to the right of the church and go through a wall gap onto a track. The small church, noted for its saddleback tower, is Norman in origin, enlarged over succeeding centuries and restored by the Victorians.

Immediately turn right **G** through a kissing-gate, at a public footpath sign to Chorleywood, walk along a path and cross a tarmac drive to a kissing-gate. Passing through it, bear right and head downhill along the right edge of a field to a gate. On the other side, keep ahead along a track to a T-junction and turn left along a track to a lane. Cross over, go through a kissing-gate opposite and walk along the right edge of a field.

In the field corner, turn right to keep by the left inside edge of woodland and continue across a boardwalk to cross a footbridge over the River Chess. From here there are lovely views both up and down the river. At a T-junction turn left, here picking up the outward route, and retrace your steps to the start. ●

Ware, Stanstead Abbotts and Great Amwell

		GPS waypoints	
Start	Ware		
Distance	6¼ miles (10km)	✎	TL 356 143
Height gain	165 feet (50m)	Ⓐ	TL 359 141
		Ⓑ	TL 369 133
Approximate time	3 hours	Ⓒ	TL 382 118
Parking	Ware	Ⓓ	TL 388 121
Ordnance Survey maps	Explorer 194 (Hertford & Bishop's	Ⓔ	TL 379 117
	Stortford), Landranger 166	Ⓕ	TL 371 126
	(Luton & Hertford)	Ⓖ	TL 366 131

Virtually the whole of this relaxing and interesting walk is beside water. The first half from Ware to Stanstead Abbotts is by the River Lea and the return is initially beside the New River. Soon after passing through the quiet village of Great Amwell, you return to the Lea for the final leg.

The town centre of Ware has a wide range of buildings, both timber-framed and brick-built, dating from the 16th to the 19th centuries. One unusual feature is that the former town houses in High Street, which runs parallel to the River Lea, had gazebos overhanging the river and a number of these survive.

✎ The walk begins by the imposing, mainly 15th-century church and the war memorial. Facing the church, turn right, follow the main road to the right

River Lea near Ware

to cross the bridge over the River Lea and immediately turn left onto a tarmac riverside path Ⓐ. Keep along the pleasant, mainly tree-lined riverbank for 2½ miles (4km) – passing Hardmead Lock Ⓑ and later Stanstead Lock – and about ¼ mile (400m) beyond Stanstead Lock, bear right up to a road Ⓒ. Turn left over the bridge for a detour into Stanstead Abbotts – plenty of pubs and cafés – curving left to see the 15th-century church Ⓓ.

Retrace your steps to the bridge over the Lea Ⓒ, go over a level crossing and in front of a bridge, turn right through a kissing-gate onto the New River Path Ⓔ. The New River is a conduit, built in the early 17th century between Great Amwell and London to improve the water supply to the capital. Keep along this path to Great Amwell and just after going through a kissing-gate, turn left to cross a footbridge over the river. Climb steps through trees into the churchyard and pass to the left of the church. Parts of this interesting Norman building date back as far as the 11th century. The tower was built in the 15th century.

At a footpath post, turn right onto a path to the right of railings along the left edge of the churchyard and follow it around right and left bends to emerge onto a lane opposite the **George IV** pub. Cross over, take the enclosed path opposite, descend steps to a lane and turn right to recross the New River. To the right, on an island in the river surrounded by weeping willows – a delightful spot – is an urn erected in 1800 to commemorate Sir Hugh Myddleton. An inscription states that he built the New River between 1609 and 1613 for the 'conveying of health, pleasure and convenience to the

Great Amwell

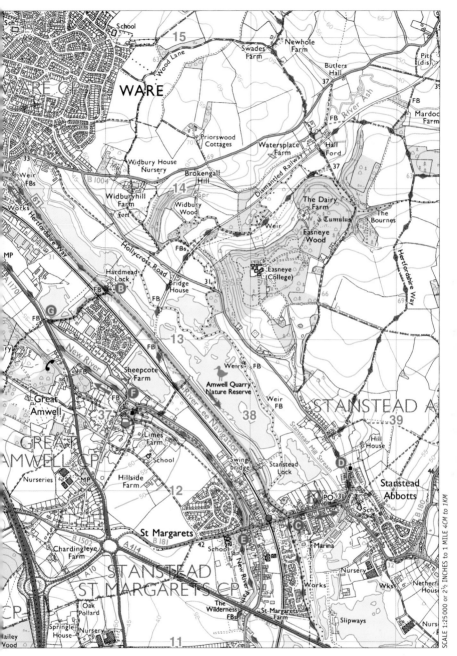

metropolis of Great Britain'.

After crossing the river, turn left through a kissing-gate **F** to continue beside it again as far as the next road bridge. Cross over the road and turn right **G** along an enclosed track. Climb a stile, carefully cross a railway line,

climb another stile and keep ahead to the River Lea **B**. Turn left, here rejoining the outward route, and retrace your steps to the start. ●

Turvey

			GPS waypoints
Start	Turvey Bridge		🖊 SP 936 524
Distance	7 miles (11.1km)		Ⓐ SP 944 524
Height gain	360 feet (110m)		Ⓑ SP 954 521
Approximate time	3 hours		Ⓒ SP 959 510
Parking	Lay-by on west (Buckinghamshire) side of Turvey Bridge		Ⓓ SP 953 493
			Ⓔ SP 940 494
Ordnance Survey maps	Explorer 208 (Bedford & St Neots), Landranger 153 (Bedford & Huntingdon)		Ⓕ SP 944 515

Fine views are enjoyed on this gently undulating route in the valley of the Great Ouse on the Bedfordshire – Buckinghamshire border. The walk explores the country to the south of the attractive village of Turvey and goes across part of Abbey Park, created in the late 18th century.

🖊 Begin by crossing the 11-arched, 13th-century Turvey Bridge over the Great Ouse, passing **Ye Three Fyshes** pub into the village. Turvey is a most attractive village and the large and impressive medieval church, restored in the 19th century, retains earlier Saxon work in the nave and tower.

Follow the road through the village and at the far end, turn right along Jacks Lane Ⓐ which narrows to a track. Bear left off the track at a cattle-grid, go through a gate and bear slightly left along a path which continues to the left of a wire fence, to a stile. Over to the left Turvey Abbey, an early 17th-century manor house, can be seen.

Climb the stile, cross a footbridge and keep ahead, by a stream on the left, to a kissing-gate. Do not go through but bear right, pass to the left of a circle of young trees and continue across Abbey Park to a stile. Until the late 18th century the park was open farmland but was enclosed and landscaped by the Higgins family of Turvey Abbey. Climb

the stile, walk across the next field, climb another stile, keep ahead to go through a fence gap and turn right along a tree-lined track Ⓑ.

The track curves left and then right to continue along the left edge of woodland and at a footpath post, bear right to cross a bridge over a disused railway. Bear left along the left edge of a field, follow it to the right and continue along a track which keeps by the wavy field edges before becoming a broad, grassy enclosed track. Where it meets a stony track at a footpath post, turn right along a track Ⓒ. The track continues along the edges of a succession of fields to reach a footpath post. Just before it turn right along the left field edge, follow the track around a left bend and turn right in the field corner Ⓓ to continue along the right edge of Ramacre Wood. Go through a gap and keep along the left edge of the next field to a lane.

Turn right, at a T-junction turn right again and at a Circular Route post where the lane curves left Ⓔ, keep ahead along a broad, grassy track across fields. Cross a track, walk on, later keeping by the winding left field edge, and at a footpath post, turn sharp left to continue along the edge. In the corner turn right to continue by the right edge of woodland, descend to pass through a hedge gap, continue downhill and go through another hedge gap. Head uphill to keep by the left edge of a field again and at the top, keep ahead along a tarmac track.

Cross a bridge over the disused railway line again and as the track curves left, Turvey church tower can be seen to the right. At public footpath and Circular Route signs, turn right ⒡ through a hedge gap and across a plank footbridge and head downhill along the left edge of a field. Go through a gap, continue along the left field edge, climb a stile in the corner and bear left across a field to climb another one. Continue across the next field, climb a stile and walk along a hedge - and tree-lined path to a road. Turn right into Turvey and at a T-junction, turn left and recross the bridge to return to the start. ●

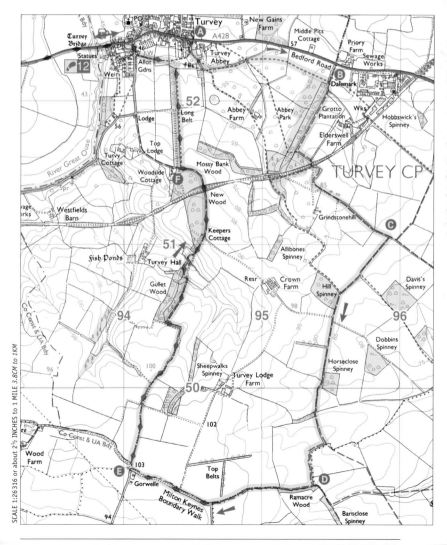

Dunstable Downs and Totternhoe

		GPS waypoints
Start	Dunstable Downs Chilterns Gateway Centre, near Robertson Corner, off B4541	🖎 TL 007 195
		Ⓐ TL 007 213
		Ⓑ SP 998 221
Distance	5¼ miles (8.3km)	Ⓒ SP 988 208
Height gain	515 feet (155m)	Ⓓ SP 998 204
Approximate time	2½ hours	Ⓔ TL 005 202
Parking	Robertson Corner	Ⓕ TL 004 196
Ordnance Survey maps	Explorers 181 (Chiltern Hills North), 192 (Buckingham & Milton Keynes) and 193 (Luton & Stevenage), Landrangers 165 (Aylesbury & Leighton Buzzard) and 166 (Luton & Hertford)	

On the first part of the walk along the Chilterns escarpment, there are superb and extensive views over the Vale of Aylesbury. After descending from the downs to the edge of Dunstable, the route continues along broad tracks into the village of Totternhoe. Field paths and enclosed tracks lead to the foot of the downs and a short climb brings you back to the start.

🖎 Start by the Dunstable Downs Chilterns Gateway Centre, face the view and descend diagonally right across grass to an Icknield Way footpath post. Turn right and take the path across the top of the downs, keeping by a wire fence on the left and following the regular Icknield Way signs. Go through a kissing-gate, keep ahead and the path veers slightly left to a fork.

Take the left-hand path and as you continue across the top of the downs, there are fine views ahead and to the left across the Vale of Aylesbury and to the right of the built-up area of Dunstable and Luton. At the next waymarked post, bear right, passing to the left of the Five Knolls, a group of round barrows built around 4000 years ago and belonging to either the late Neolithic or early Bronze Age. Descend

to go through a kissing-gate and continue downhill across grass to reach a road on the edge of Dunstable Ⓐ.

Cross the road by a small roundabout and keep ahead along a wide, enclosed, grassy track for ¾ mile (1.2km) as far as a crossways. Turn left Ⓑ along another wide, enclosed, grassy track which emerges onto a road in Totternhoe. Take the lane ahead (Furlong Lane) and turn left at a T-junction, passing to the left of the **Old Farm Inn** and the 15th-century church. At a public footpath sign, turn left and go through a kissing-gate Ⓒ. Walk diagonally across the top end of a field to climb a three-bar fence at a public footpath sign before making for a short line of trees where you cross a footbridge. Continue diagonally across the next field onto a lane at a bend.

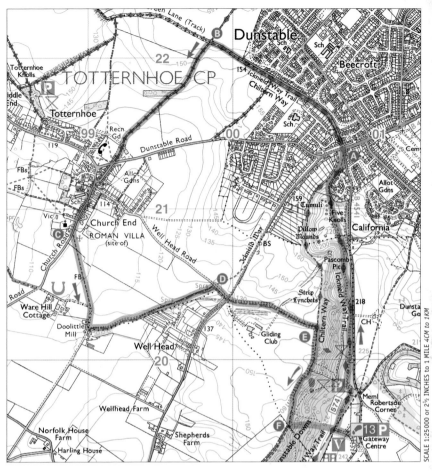

SCALE 1:25000 or 2½ INCHES to 1 MILE 4CM to 1KM

Walk footpath post. Turn left **F** and head up the slope of the downs to return to the start. ●

Turn left and just before a farm, turn left, at a public bridleway sign, along an enclosed track to a gate. Go through, keep ahead along a broad, enclosed track – there is a stream on the right – and go through a gate onto a lane **D**. Turn right to a T-junction and continue along the enclosed track ahead which later heads gently uphill to the foot of the downs. After going through a gate, turn right **E** along a path which runs along the foot of the downs to a gate. The field beyond the fence on the right is used by the London Gliding Club.

Go through the gate and keep ahead along an enclosed path to a Circular

Dunstable Downs

Odell, Great Wood and Harrold

Odell, Great Wood and Harrold

		GPS waypoints
Start	Harrold Odell Country Park	🖉 SP 956 566
Distance	5¾ miles (9.2km)	Ⓐ SP 965 577
Height gain	260 feet (80m)	Ⓑ SP 960 589
Approximate time	2¾ hours	Ⓒ SP 963 595
Parking	Harrold Odell Country Park	Ⓓ SP 952 596
Ordnance Survey maps	Explorer 208 (Bedford & St Neots), Landranger 153 (Bedford & Huntingdon)	Ⓔ SP 948 582
		Ⓕ SP 952 568

This pleasant walk begins by the lakes of the Harrold Odell Country Park and includes two attractive stone villages and a fine area of ancient woodland. It is an easy-paced and well-waymarked route and there are splendid views across the valley of the Great Ouse. Expect some of the paths and tracks, especially through Odell Great Wood, to be muddy at times.

Harrold Odell Country Park, situated in the valley of the Great Ouse, is an attractive mixture of lakes, river, woodland and meadows and was created from land used for sand and gravel extraction.

🖉 Start by walking along the straight, well-surfaced track that bisects the two lakes and continues along the right shore of the larger lake. After passing beside a gate, keep ahead along a lane through the small stone-built village of Odell.

At a junction by the village green (**The Bell**, right) Ⓐ, continue along the main road, follow it around a right bend and just before the 15th-century church, turn left beside a gate, at a public bridleway sign, and walk along a straight, broad, tree-lined track. The track passes a gate and continues through Odell Great Wood, the largest block of ancient woodland in the area,

The attractive village of Odell

which mainly comprises oak and ash. At a footpath post at a seven-way junction of tracks and paths, bear right **B** (in the direction of a public footpath sign) along another straight but narrower track.

After emerging from the trees, the track continues towards a farm. Cross a track, pass to the right of the farm buildings, keep ahead along the right edge of a field, pass to the right of a pool and go through a hedge gap to a T-junction. Turn left **C** along a wide,

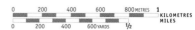

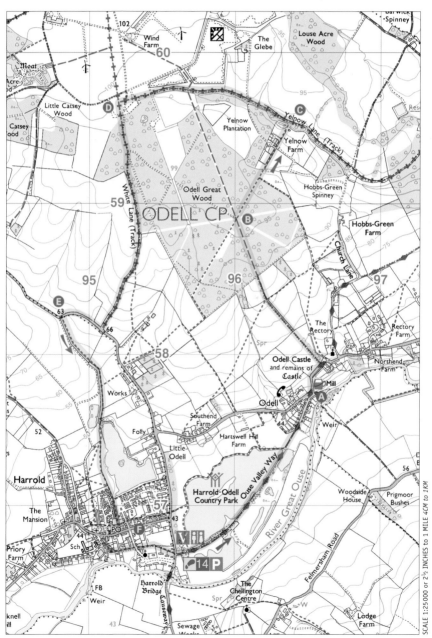

Circular lock-up in Harrold

enclosed track which continues along the right inside edge of the wood to a crossways. To the right is the disused Podington airfield, used by American forces during the Second World War. Keep ahead, crossing one of the former runways, bear right to a T-junction and turn left **D**, in the Harrold direction, along an enclosed track (White Lane). Cross another runway, continue through Great Wood again and after emerging from the trees, keep ahead along a wide, enclosed track to a road.

Turn right and where the road bends right, turn left **E**. Pass beside a barrier, continue to a public footpath sign, and walk along the right edge of a field. Go through a kissing-gate, continue along the field edge with the stream and a wire fence on your right, then go through a second kissing-gate. Keep ahead to cross a footbridge over a stream where it cascades down into a lake. Keep ahead along a tree-lined path, bear right to go through a kissing-gate, turn left and

walk along the left edge of a field, going through two gates. After going through a kissing-gate, the route continues along an enclosed path.

Turn left to cross a stream, then immediately turn right to continue along an enclosed path beside it and the path bends left to join a tarmac path. Continue along it to a road in Harrold, turn right (Dove Lane) into the village and at a crossroads, turn right **F** along the village street to the attractive green. The two buildings on the green are a late 17th-century or early 18th-century octagonal market house and an early 19th-century circular stone lock-up.

Turn left onto a tarmac path along the left edge of the green and continue along an enclosed tarmac path – the Great Ouse is to the right – which bends left towards the mainly 13th-century church. Cross a drive, keep ahead and go through a kissing-gate into the churchyard. Walk along a tarmac path which bears right to emerge, via a kissing-gate, onto the road opposite the entrance to the country park. ●

Sundon Hills and Sharpenhoe Clappers

Start	Sundon Hills Country Park, on minor road between Harlington and Upper Sundon
Distance	5 miles (8.2km)
Height gain	665 feet (205m)
Approximate time	2½ hours
Parking	Sundon Hills Country Park
Ordnance Survey maps	Explorer 193 (Luton & Stevenage), Landranger 166 (Luton & Hertford)

GPS waypoints

- 🖉 TL 047 285
- Ⓐ TL 061 290
- Ⓑ TL 065 295
- Ⓒ TL 066 301
- Ⓓ TL 065 306
- Ⓔ TL 063 301

The first part of the walk is along the ridge of the Sundon Hills, from where there are dramatic views both of the wooded hillside of Sharpenhoe Clappers and the surrounding Bedfordshire countryside. After heading up to the beeches that crown the summit of Sharpenhoe Clappers, you descend to the village of Sharpenhoe and continue along the base of the hills before climbing through woodland and retracing your steps along the ridge to the start.

The chalk slopes of the Sundon Hills – quite steep by Bedfordshire standards – are an eastern extension of the main Chiltern range and rise to over 500 feet (152m) above the surrounding countryside, giving superb and extensive views. They are thought to be the 'Delectable Mountains' of John Bunyan's *The Pilgrim's Progress.*

The first half of the walk is particularly well-waymarked as most of it follows three long-distance footpaths – Bunyan Trail, Chiltern Way and Icknield Way Path.

🖉 Begin from the far right of the car park and go through a metal kissing-gate. Now follows a superb ridge walk as you

Sharpenhoe Clappers

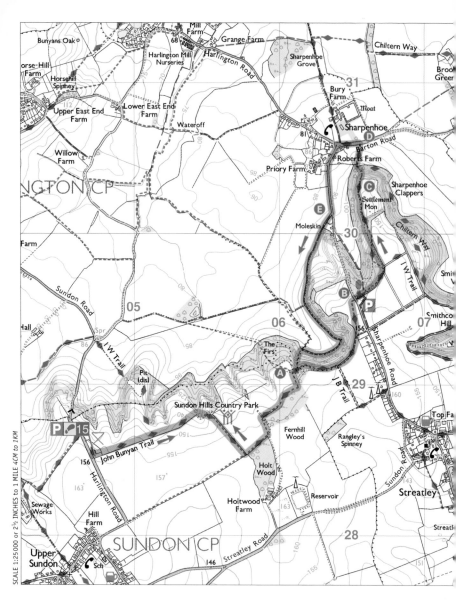

SCALE 1:25000 or 2½ INCHES to 1 MILE 4CM to 1KM

| 0 | 200 | 400 | 600 | 800 METRES | 1 |
| 0 | 200 | 400 | 600 YARDS | ½ | KILOMETRES MILES |

keep along the top of the hills, by a fence and hedge on the right, enjoying magnificent views of the Sharpenhoe Clappers ahead and over a large slice of Bedfordshire to the left.

Go through a kissing-gate, turn right along an enclosed track which bends left and after passing through a hedge gap, do not continue ahead but turn right to a kissing-gate. Go through,

walk along the left edge of a field and in the corner, turn left through a gap and continue along the right edge of the next field, by woodland on the right. At the corner of the wood, bear slightly left by a waymarked post along a track to the corner of the next woodland, bear left along its left edge and at the next corner, turn right to continue by the left edge of the wood.

In the field corner, turn left and look out for where a waymarked post directs you to turn right into the wood. Turn right at the next fingerpost and keep ahead along a wooded ridge – there are some beautiful old beeches – to a stile. Climb it, keep ahead along an undulating path which bends left to another stile, turn right over it, walk across a field, go through a kissing-gate and descend steps to a road . Cross over to Sharpenhoe Clappers car park, pass beside two gates in quick succession and walk along a tarmac track to redundant gateposts. Keep ahead along an enclosed path by woodland on the left, and at the next footpath post, bear left to continue along the right edge of woodland. At this point you leave the Icknield Way Path but keep on the Bunyan Trail.

Bear right on joining another path, take the right-hand path at a fork and at the next fork – just after entering woodland – take the left-hand path up to the summit of Sharpenhoe Clappers , site of an Iron Age fort and crowned by beech trees that were planted in the 1830s. A monument records that the wooded hill was bequeathed to the National Trust by W.A. Robertson in memory of his brothers who died in the First World War.

Continue past the monument and on the edge of the circle of beeches, turn left and at a Chiltern Way Extension post, turn right and descend a long flight of steps. Walk along the left edge of a field to a road and turn left into Sharpenhoe. Turn left along Sharpenhoe Road and at a public bridleway sign, bear right beside a gate and walk along the left edge of a field. Ahead is a fine view of the Sundon Hills. At a footpath post in front of a National Trust sign for Moleskin and Markham Hills, bear left and follow this enclosed winding path as it skirts the edge of the wood. At a junction of paths, at a kissing-gate, turn left and head steeply uphill through woodland and climb steps to a footpath post . Keep ahead, here rejoining the outward route, and retrace your steps, following the regular waymarks, to the start. ●

Sharpenhoe Clappers

Whitwell and St Paul'sWalden

		GPS waypoints
Start	Whitwell	 TL 184 211
Distance	5¾ miles (9.1km)	Ⓐ TL 187 210
Height gain	425 feet (130m)	Ⓑ TL 192 222
Approximate time	2¾ hours	Ⓒ TL 199 234
Parking	Roadside parking at Whitwell	Ⓓ TL 212 224
Ordnance Survey maps	Explorer 193 (Luton & Stevenage), Landranger 166 (Luton & Hertford)	Ⓔ TL 202 217

A gentle climb out of the Mimram valley, passing the medieval church of St Paul's Walden, is followed by a delightful walk across fields, through woods and along quiet lanes. There are fine views over the surrounding countryside and the last stretch is along a tree- and hedge-lined track called Nortonstreet Lane.

The walk begins in Whitwell's High Street, an attractive mixture of houses and cottages of all styles and ages, by the village stores. Facing the shop, walk right, soon passing **The Bull** (left), and shortly afterwards at a public footpath sign, turn left Ⓐ along a track between houses. Turn left in front of a brick building, go through a kissing-gate and walk across a small field to cross a footbridge over the little River Mimram.

Countryside near Whitwell

Go through a kissing-gate, cross a track, and head uphill along an enclosed grassy path. At the top, go through a kissing-gate, keep ahead to go through two gates in quick succession and continue along the right edge of a field. The large house seen over to the left is St Paul's Walden Bury, birthplace of the late Queen Mother in 1900. After going through a kissing-gate, bear right along an attractive, tree-lined, tarmac drive and at a fork, take the left-hand track which continues uphill to a lane opposite the fine, battlemented, flint church of St Paul's Walden Ⓑ. This dates mainly from the 14th and 15th centuries, though the chancel was remodelled in the 18th century. St Paul's Walden is only a hamlet but there is a pub, the **Strathmore Arms**, a short distance to the right.

Cross the lane, go through a gate into the churchyard, pass to the right of the church and go through another gate onto a tarmac track. Turn left and at a public footpath sign, turn right along a narrow, enclosed path which emerges into a field. Continue along its right edge to a hedge corner, keep ahead to the right of a fence and on the far side, go through a hedge gap onto a road. Turn left and at a public footpath sign just beyond the gates of Stagenhoe (a Sue Ryder Home), turn right along a track through woodland. On emerging into a field, keep ahead across it – later by its right edge – to a redundant stile. Continue across the next field and climb a stile onto a lane  **C**. Turn right along this pleasant, shady lane to a T-junction and turn left. Follow the lane around a right

bend and after ¾ mile (1.2km), turn right **D** at a public bridleway sign, along a track by the right edge of a field. The track curves right in the field corner and on entering the next field, keep straight ahead across it. Continue through woodland and then along the left edge of a field to a lane, turn right and where the lane bends right, turn left, at a public byway sign **E**, along a hedge- and tree-lined track.

The track – Nortonstreet Lane – goes round several bends, later narrows to a path and heads downhill to a road. Turn right to return to the start. ●

SCALE 1:25000 or 2½ INCHES to 1 MILE 4CM to 1KM

```
0    200   400   600   800 METRES  1
                                      KILOMETRES
                                      MILES
0    200   400   600 YARDS    ½
```

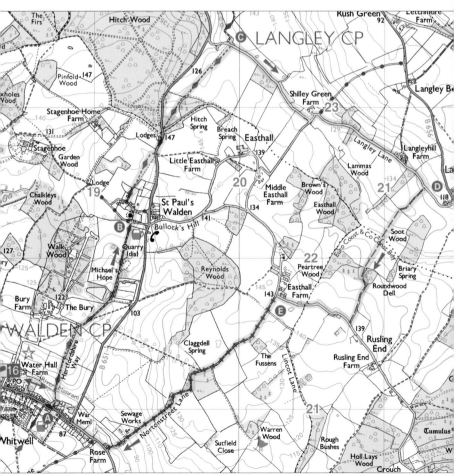

Chipperfield and Kings Langley

		GPS waypoints
Start	Chipperfield, car park facing the common	 TL 044 015
Distance	6½ miles (10.5km)	Ⓐ TL 049 012
Height gain	480 feet (145m)	Ⓑ TL 079 020
		Ⓒ TL 077 020
Approximate time	3 hours	Ⓓ TL 076 027
Parking	Chipperfield	Ⓔ TL 071 029
Ordnance Survey maps	Explorer 182 (St Albans & Hatfield), Landranger 166 (Luton & Hertford)	Ⓕ TL 052 033
		Ⓖ TL 045 020

The walk takes you across two of the wooded commons that are a feature of this part of Hertfordshire. From Chipperfield Common, the route heads across fields before descending into the Gade valley to the Grand Union Canal. A short walk by the canal is followed by a gentle climb through Kings Langley and across its common. There are fine views over the surrounding countryside before the final leg through the delightful Scatterdells Wood.

Chipperfield is a most attractive village with houses, church and pub grouped around a cricket field and overlooking the thickly wooded common. The church is Victorian, built in 1838 and enlarged in the 1880s.

🖉 Begin by facing the common and turning left along the road. You can continue along the road and pick up the route at point Ⓐ but *for a more attractive opening stretch, bear right along a path, at an Easy Access Route sign, to head through the superb woodland of the common. At Apostles Pond, bear left and then, almost immediately, bear left again. Cross a track and keep ahead to rejoin the road* Ⓐ.

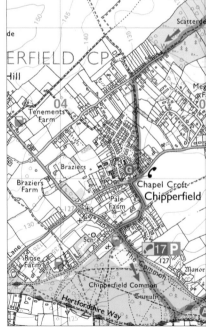

0	200	400	600	800 METRES	1
					KILOMETRES
					MILES
0	200	400	600 YARDS	½	

Grand Union Canal at Kings Langley

kissing-gate, keep ahead to go through another gate, walk along the track and go through two more kissing-gates in quick succession. Continue along an enclosed path, go through a kissing-gate, walk along the left edge of a field and keep ahead to another kissing-gate. Go through and walk along the right edge of a field, use a kissing-gate and continue along the left edge of a field. Go through two more kissing-gates in quick succession, and continue along an enclosed path signposted to Kings Langley.

Cross over and at a public footpath sign to Kings Langley, take the enclosed path to the left of a tarmac track. This part of the route follows both the Hertfordshire Way and a Grand Union Canal Circular Walk. Go through a

On reaching the end of the path, go through a kissing-gate and veer slightly left across a field to pass through

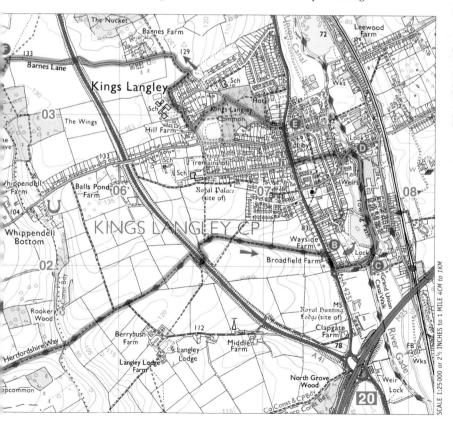

Chipperfield

another. Head straight out across the ensuing field. Halfway over, take the right diagonal path to meet and climb an embankment; go through a kissing-gate and cross a footbridge over the A41.

Turn left and the path bears right to a kissing-gate. Go through and head gently downhill along the left edge of a field. Continue down the track at the field edge and then go through a gate in the bottom-left corner. Walk along an enclosed track, go through a gate by a farm and keep ahead through a kissing-gate and on down to a main road on the edge of Kings Langley **B**. Turn right and just before reaching a road on the left, turn left along an enclosed path, signed 'Station Footpath'. Where this path ends, keep ahead between embankments and turn left along the towpath of the Grand Union Canal **C**.

The towpath runs between the canal on the right and the River Gade on the left and on the opposite bank of the canal is the site of the original Ovaltine factory, established there in 1913. At the first bridge, head up to a road **D**, turn left, take the first road on the right (Water Side) and at a public footpath sign, turn left onto an enclosed tarmac path. Continue along it, crossing several side roads, up to the High Street. On the way, the tower and spire of Kings Langley's medieval church is seen to the

left. Inside is the tomb of Edmund de Langley, one of the sons of Edward III.

Turn right along the High Street, turn left along Common Lane **E** and after ¹/₂ mile (800m) at a public footpath sign, bear left into the woodland of Kings Langley Common. Keep straight ahead, then take the first footpath on the right, signposted 'Love Lane'. Keep ahead at all path junctions and, after emerging from the trees, continue along the right edge of a cricket field to a road. Turn right and just before the road bends right, turn left towards the entrance to Kings Langley School. In front of the school gates, turn right along an enclosed path and follow this path around the edge of the school grounds, first round a right bend and then two left bends, before turning right beside steps onto a narrow lane.

Turn left, passing under the A41, and after just over ¹/₂ mile (800m), turn left through a gate **F**, at a public footpath sign, and head across a field towards woodland. After going through a kissing-gate follow a path through the delightful Scatterdells Wood, heading down into a dip and up again. Continue through the wood to pass through a gate on the far side and keep ahead along a lane.

At a public footpath sign to Chapel Croft, turn left along an enclosed path, cross a track and continue in a straight line along an enclosed wooded path to a road **G**. Turn right into Chipperfield, take the enclosed path parallel to the first road on the left (Kings Lane), rejoin the road and follow it around a right bend and at a crossroads, with the **Two Brewers** pub ahead, turn left to the start. ●

Northchurch Common and the Grand Union Canal

Start	Berkhamsted	**GPS waypoints**	
Distance	6 miles (9.7km)	🖉	SP 991 077
Height gain	395 feet (120m)	Ⓐ	SP 992 081
Approximate time	3 hours	Ⓑ	SP 978 095
		Ⓒ	SP 970 106
Parking	Berkhamsted	Ⓓ	SP 965 097
Ordnance Survey maps	Explorer 181 (Chiltern Hills North), Landranger 165 (Aylesbury & Leighton Buzzard)		

This is the second walk in this guide that takes you across part of the National Trust's Ashridge Estate. From Berkhamsted the route heads up onto the expanses of Northchurch Common, a superb combination of open grassland and thick woodland with fine views over the Bulbourne valley. The return is a relaxing stroll beside the Grand Union Canal.

Berkhamsted lies in a valley that has always been a major routeway through the Chilterns from London to the Midlands and North – the Grand Union Canal, a busy railway line and a main road pass through it. The Normans recognised Berkhamsted's strategic importance and built the castle; much

Grand Union Canal near Berkhamsted

of the later stonework of this once important fortress and royal residence has vanished to reveal the 11th-century earthworks of the original, simple motte-and-bailey construction. Berkhamsted also has a large 13th-century church and, despite much modern development, retains some attractive old cottages.

🖉 Start in High Street by the 19th-century former town hall and, facing it, turn left. Take the first road on the right, cross a bridge over the canal and the road bends right to the station. Turn left, in the Ashridge and Potten End direction, to pass under a railway bridge – Berkhamsted Castle is to the right – turn left into Bridgewater Road and take the first road on the right (Castle Hill Avenue) Ⓐ. Head uphill and where the road bends left, keep ahead, at a public footpath sign, along an enclosed path.

Bear left along a road and at a public footpath sign, bear right along a track. At a fork, take the right-hand track, keep ahead at a public footpath sign, take the right-hand track at the next fork and continue up to climb a stile. Walk along the left edge of a field, go through a kissing-gate, continue along an enclosed path and go through a kissing-gate to a crossways. Keep ahead along an enclosed track in front of houses to a fork on the edge of woodland and take the left-hand tarmac track, heading downhill through trees. Where the track bends sharply left, keep ahead across grass and continue uphill Ⓑ along a grassy ride through the woodlands of Northchurch Common.

Cross a tarmac track, keep ahead, bear slightly left on emerging into an open area and follow a clear grassy track to a road. Cross over, continue along the undulating path opposite and after a waymarked post, cross a track and keep ahead along a broad green ride. Keep ahead at a crossways and on emerging into a large open area of grassland, turn left along its left edge. At a crossways in the corner of this grassy area Ⓒ, turn left and on emerging from the trees, keep ahead downhill along a narrow lane. Take the first lane on the right – this is even narrower – follow it around a left bend, cross a railway bridge and continue to a T-junction.

Turn left parallel to the canal and at the next T-junction, turn right to cross a bridge and turn left onto the towpath

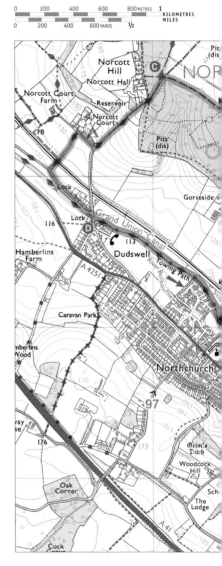

Northchurch Common

of the Grand Union Canal . Follow the towpath back to Berkhamsted, passing several locks, and later the little River Bulbourne is seen to the right. At a Grand Union Canal Circular Walk waymark by a painted bridge, veer right and follow the winding path to the left of Waitrose to the road and retrace your steps to the start of the walk.

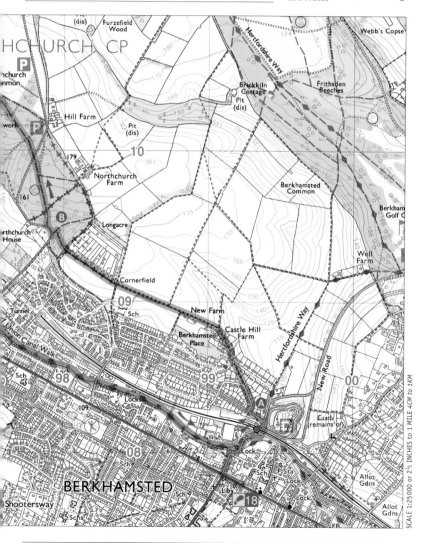

SCALE 1:25000 or 2½ INCHES to 1 MILE 4CM to 1KM

Barkway, Reed and Earl's Wood

Start	Barkway
Distance	6¼ miles (9.9km)
Height gain	300 feet (90m)
Approximate time	3 hours
Parking	Roadside parking at Barkway
Ordnance Survey maps	Explorer 194 (Hertford & Bishop's Stortford), Landranger 154 (Cambridge & Newmarket)

GPS waypoints

🖉 TL 384 356
Ⓐ TL 383 359
Ⓑ TL 364 360
Ⓒ TL 361 357
Ⓓ TL 378 354
Ⓔ TL 383 352
Ⓕ TL 399 350
Ⓖ TL 393 356

This figure-of-eight walk is based around the village of Barkway and can obviously be split into two, separate shorter routes. Both Barkway and Reed are attractive villages, there are wide views across the surrounding countryside of east Hertfordshire and much enjoyable walking either beside or through woodland.

Barkway's attractive High Street is a varied collection of houses and cottages from all periods and the walk begins opposite Church Lane.

🖉 The first part of the figure-of-eight route is between Barkway and Reed. Facing Church Lane, turn right and walk up High Street through the village and turn left along Royston Road. Where it bends right, keep ahead, at a public byway sign, along an enclosed path Ⓐ.

The path continues along the left edge of a field to a fork by a footpath post. Take the left-hand path which keeps by the left edge of a field and later along the right edge of Rokey Wood. At the corner of the wood, the route continues ahead along a well-surfaced track. Where this track bends right, keep ahead to pass through a belt of trees and continue across fields to a track. Turn right and continue as it bends left then right. Turn left and go through two kissing-gates in quick succession, and head towards the left field edge. Go through a kissing-gate onto a lane Ⓑ. Turn left on to High Street in Reed and turn right into Driftway to a T-junction. Turn left and where the lane bends right, turn left, at a public footpath sign, and go through a

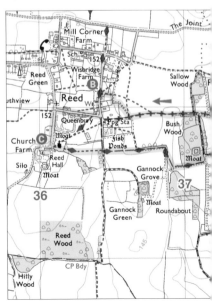

Barkway village sign

gate into Reed churchyard **C**. Pass to the right of the medieval church, go through a hedge gap, cross a plank footbridge and walk across a field. On the far side, cross a track, follow a faint path into the trees – this is not easy to spot – cross a footbridge and head up the embankment in front. Keep in a straight line across a field. On the far

side continue along a track, follow it around a right bend and at a hedge corner, turn left into a field.

Turn half-right, head diagonally across the field to a T-junction by a footpath post and turn left along a

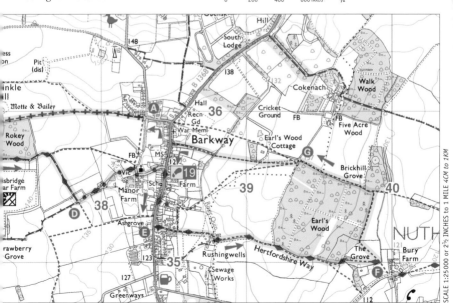

Reed church

track. The track later keeps along the right edge of Bush Wood, bends left at the corner of the wood and then bends right to continue across fields. It then keeps along the right edge of Rokey Wood and at the corner of the wood, keep ahead, first along a tree-lined path and then along an enclosed track that curves right and continues, to a T-junction **D**. Turn left along a track to a T-junction in front of Barkway church, a large, mainly 15th-century structure, restored in the Victorian era. Turn right and the track bends left to emerge into High Street at the start.

For the second part of the figure-of-eight walk – between Barkway and Earl's Wood – turn right and after ¹/₄ mile (400m), turn left, at a public footpath sign, along an enclosed path **E**. Follow it around right and left bends and continue to a T-junction. Turn right along a tarmac track and where the road bends right continue ahead past a waymarked post, follow the path to the left of a barn conversion and head to the right and at a footpath post, turn left along a track by the edge of a field. The track continues along the right edge of Earl's Wood and at the corner of the wood, follow the path around a left bend to a kissing-gate. Go through, bear right to a fence corner and continue across the field to a kissing-gate **F**. Do not go through it but turn sharp left, head back across the field towards Earl's Wood and go through a kissing-gate in the corner.

Walk along the left edge of a field and in the corner, turn left along a track. Pass through a belt of trees and the track continues by the right edge of Earl's Wood again. At the corner of the wood **G**, bear slightly left and head across a field, making for the corner of the trees and bushes seen ahead. Continue across the field and on the far side, keep ahead along an attractive, tree-lined path which emerges onto High Street in Barkway. Turn left to return to the start. ●

Upper Lea valley and Someries Castle

		GPS waypoints	
Start	Peter's Green		TL 142 190
Distance	6½ miles (10.5km)	**A**	TL 137 189
Height gain	465 feet (140m)	**B**	TL 131 179
Approximate time	3 hours	**C**	TL 128 172
Parking	Roadside parking at Peter's Green	**D**	TL 127 170
Ordnance Survey maps	Explorers 182 (St Albans & Hatfield) and 193 (Luton & Stevenage), Landranger 166 (Luton & Hertford)	**E**	TL 119 183
		F	TL 111 200
		G	TL 135 193

The route falls into three distinct parts. First comes a gentle descent into the Lea valley, with fine views ahead. Then follows a walk through the valley, pleasantly wooded at times, mainly along a former railway track to the southern outskirts of Luton. Finally, a gradual climb up to the sparse remains of Someries Castle and then a track and lane bring you back to the start.

The walk starts at the green by the **Bright Star** pub. With your back to the pub walk ahead along the road signposted to Chiltern Green, and at a public footpath sign, (Chiltern Way), turn left along a path. Follow it across fields

Remains of Someries Castle

to a track **A**. Go through a kissing-gate opposite, keep ahead by the left edge of a field and climb two more kissing-gates in quick succession.

Continue across fields to a crossways by a clump of trees and turn left, at a public footpath sign, initially by the right edge of the trees and then along the right edge of a field. At a footpath post, turn right **B** and head gently downhill across fields – there are fine views ahead over the Lea valley – and at the bottom end, turn left and walk along the right field edge to a lane. Turn right down to a T-junction in East Hyde **C**, turn right and almost immediately turn left along Thrales End Lane. Cross a bridge over the River Lea and just after passing under a railway bridge, turn right **D** – here joining the Lea Valley Walk – and walk along the right edge of a field below the railway embankment.

The next part of the route is mostly along the track of the former Luton, Dunstable and Welwyn Junction Railway, completed in 1860 and closed in 1965. The parallel present line was opened in 1868. Where the field edge veers slightly left, keep ahead along an enclosed path to a footpath post, turn right down steps and turn left to continue along a woodland path which may be overgrown. The stout metal fence on the right is the boundary fence of a sewage works. At a footpath post, bear right to descend steps and continue along a path onto a road.

Go through the barrier diagonally opposite, walk along an enclosed path, recross the river and bear right to climb a stile. Descend steps, and turn sharp left to a road **E**. Cross carefully, go through a barrier diagonally opposite, ascend steps and continue through woodland, first along the top of an embankment and later through a wooded cutting. Cross a lane and go through a kissing-gate. As you continue along the right field edge, below the present railway embankment, the great parkland surrounding Luton Hoo – an 18th-century country house, remodelled both in the 19th and early 20th centuries – can be seen over to the left.

Just before the path starts to descend, bear left and head downhill across a field towards the road again, passing to the left of a wooded section of former embankment, to a track. Cross it, and keep ahead by the right edge of a field and at the far tapering end of the field, go through a kissing-gate onto the road. Keep ahead and in a few paces turn right **F** under a railway bridge, walk along a track and head across a field to a footpath post at the corner of a wire fence.

Here you leave the Lea Valley Walk by keeping ahead along the left edge of a field, below an embankment which borders Luton Airport and following Circular Walk waymarks. At a way-marked post, continue uphill along the right side of a wire fence, and continue

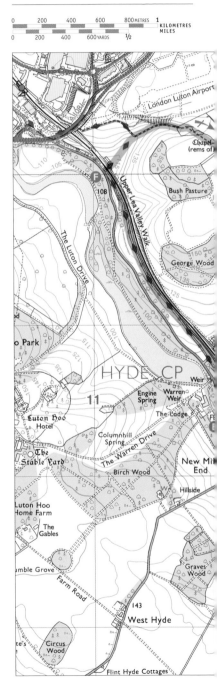

to a kissing-gate. Go through and head across to the ruins of Someries Castle. All that is left of this 15th-century manor house, one of the earliest brick structures in England, is the gatehouse and chapel.

Walk along the track, between the ruins on the right and a farm on the left, go through a kissing-gate and bear right along a broad track. This later becomes a lane which you follow to a T-junction **G**. Turn right along a road to another T-junction, turn right again and at a public bridleway sign, turn left along a track. On reaching a stile on the right **A**, turn left to retrace your steps to Peter's Green. ●

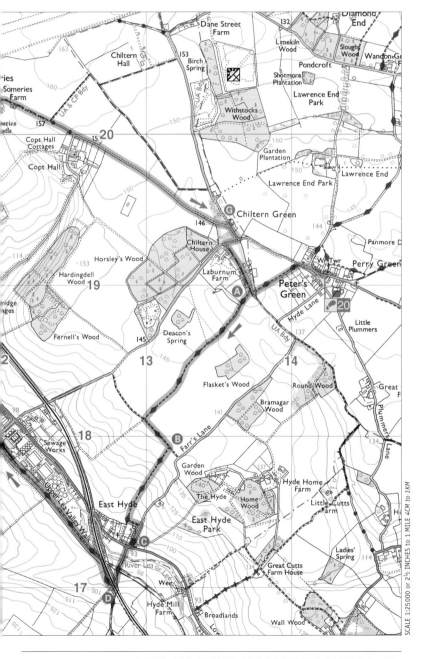

SCALE 1:25000 or 2½ INCHES to 1 MILE 4CM to 1KM

Ardeley, Benington and Walkern

		GPS waypoints
Start	Ardeley	![] TL 310 272
Distance	7 miles (11.3km)	Ⓐ TL 305 272
Height gain	425 feet (130m)	Ⓑ TL 299 250
Approximate time	3½ hours	Ⓒ TL 298 237
Parking	Roadside parking at Ardeley	Ⓓ TL 283 239
Ordnance Survey maps	Explorers 193 (Luton & Stevenage) and 194 (Hertford & Bishop's Stortford), Landranger 166 (Luton & Hertford)	Ⓔ TL 288 262

This pleasant and undemanding route, in the gently undulating countryside of the Beane valley, passes through three of the most attractive villages in Hertfordshire. The walking is mainly across fields and through areas of woodland and there are extensive views across the valley. Despite the fact that it is only a short distance to the east of Stevenage, there is also a surprisingly timeless and remote feel about the walk.

With a fine medieval church and picturesque green, Ardeley is an exceptionally attractive village. The green, lined by thatched cottages and with a brick well in the middle, is rather deceptive. It was only created in 1917 by the Lord of the Manor to make a more idyllic scene.

![] The walk begins in front of the **Jolly Waggoner**. With your back to the pub, walk along the lane, passing to the right of the church and to the left of the green, and where the lane bends right, turn left Ⓐ along a tarmac track, at a public byway sign.

Where the tarmac ends, keep ahead along an undulating, tree-lined track and after emerging from the trees, continue along the right edge of fields. Pass through a belt of trees, follow the track to the right and at a hedge corner, turn left along an enclosed track. At a

T-junction, turn left towards a barn and at a crossways, turn right, passing to the left of the barn, along an enclosed, tarmac track to a lane at a junction. Keep ahead along this narrow lane and where it curves left in front of woodland, bear right, at a public bridleway sign, along a track which keeps by the left edge of fields, with woodland on the left.

At a lane, turn right and at a public bridleway sign, turn left along a track Ⓑ. To the left is an impressive view of the façade of Walkern Hall, built in the early 19th century. Join a tree-lined, concrete drive, follow it to a lane and turn left into the village of Benington. This is another picturesque village, with all the usual ingredients that make up the traditional English village scene – duck pond, green, timber-framed cottages, old pub

Picturesque countryside near Ardeley

- **The Bell** in Benington – and 13th- to 15th-century church. Next to the church is Benington Lordship, a Georgian house remodelled in Victorian times with neo-Norman additions, including a gatehouse, to harmonise with the scanty remains of a Norman castle.

By the parish hall – just before reaching the green – turn sharp right through a kissing-gate, at a public footpath sign to Aston End and Walkern Road ⓒ, and walk along the left edge of a field. At a fence corner, go through another kissing-gate, keep ahead across the field, cross a plank footbridge and continue across the next two fields. At the far end of the second field, pass through a hedge gap and cross a footbridge over a ditch. Walk along the right edge of a field, passing to the left of a pond, go through a kissing-gate and join a track and follow it across a field towards farm buildings.

Keep ahead along a concrete track, passing between barns, and where the track ends, keep ahead to pick up a grassy path. Go through a kissing-gate, keep along the left edge of a field, with woodland on the left, climb a stile in the field corner and continue through trees. After emerging from them, keep ahead along a narrow, enclosed path to a road ⓓ, cross over, continue across a field and cross a footbridge over the little River Beane. Follow the path to the left and at a crossways, turn right along the left edge of a field.

Follow the edge to the right, turn left through a kissing-gate, keep ahead across a field and after passing a waymarked post, the route continues by the river to another kissing-gate. Go through, keep ahead across a meadow, ford a brook, go through a gate and continue across the next meadow – do not take the path which bears right – to pass through another gate. Keep ahead to a kissing-gate, continue by the river again, go through a kissing-gate and keep by the left edge of the next meadow.

Ignoring the more obvious path which keeps ahead, look out for where you go through a kissing-gate between hedges and keep along the right edge of a field to another kissing-gate. Go through that one, continue along a track and climb a stile onto a road by an impressive former Victorian flour mill. Turn left into Walkern, larger than the other two villages and, at a junction, keep ahead along High Street. One of Walkern's claims to fame is that it was the home of Jane Wenham, the last person in England to be convicted of witchcraft, in 1711.

Turn right along a narrow lane ⓔ (Totts Lane) just before the **Yew Tree** pub, which bends first left, then right and then left again to a T-junction. Keep ahead through a kissing-gate, walk across a field towards the tower of

SCALE 1:25000 or 2½ INCHES to 1 MILE 4CM to 1KM

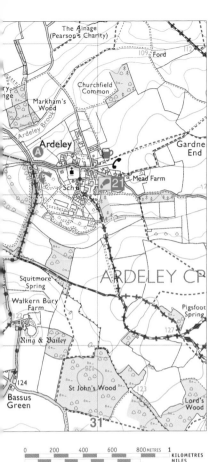

Walkern Church, go through another kissing-gate and turn right to cross a footbridge.

Keep ahead along a lane, passing to the right of the church, one of the oldest in Hertfordshire. It was founded in the 11th century and still retains some Saxon and Norman work. At a public footpath sign, turn left up steps and keep ahead to a kissing-gate. Go through, bear right across a field, continue along its left edge and in the corner, keep ahead between trees and bushes to another kissing-gate. Go through, enter a field and turn left along its left edge. The path curves first right and then left to continue along the field edge and in the corner, turn right through a belt of trees and keep along the right edge of the next field.

Climb a stile, head gently downhill along the right edge of the next two fields and in the corner of the second field, go through a gate. Continue straight across the next field, climb a stile on the far side, walk along an enclosed path to a lane and keep ahead to the start. ●

Village green, Ardeley

John Bunyan Country

		GPS waypoints
Start	Priory Country Park, about 1½ miles (2.4km) to the east of Bedford town centre	 TL 072 493
Distance	7½ miles (12.1km)	Ⓐ TL 079 489
		Ⓑ TL 084 480
Height gain	145 feet (45m)	Ⓒ TL 067 471
Approximate time	3½ hours	Ⓓ TL 065 475
Parking	Priory Country Park	Ⓔ TL 050 474
		Ⓕ TL 053 408
Ordnance Survey maps	Explorer 208 (Bedford & St Neots), Landranger 153 (Bedford & Huntingdon)	Ⓖ TL 050 495
		Ⓗ TL 062 494

A short stretch through a modern business park and a 1¼-mile (2km) walk along roads through the built-up area between Elstow and Bedford is more than compensated for by some delightful riverside walking beside the Great Ouse, two attractive villages and much historic and architectural interest. There is a strong John Bunyan theme: he was born in Elstow, wrote The Pilgrim's Progress *while in Bedford jail and there are museums and various sites associated with his life in both Elstow and Bedford.*

Start in front of the visitor centre, walk down to the lake and turn right onto the tarmac path beside it. Go through a gate, cross a drive, go through another gate and turn left along a track, between a wall on the right and a hedge on the left. At a slight fork, continue straight ahead on a grassy path, walking parallel to the wall until reaching the Great Ouse, here

The Great Ouse, Bedford

The 16th-century Moot Hall, Elstow

turning left along a riverside path.

Keep beside the river, tree-lined at times, across meadows and over several bridges. The path later becomes a tarmac one and bears right to cross first Cardington Lock Bridge and then Cardington Sluice Bridge Ⓐ. Go straight on, passing a car park (right), continue ahead along a tarmac drive to a T-junction and turn right along a road through Priory Business Park. Keep ahead at a roundabout, turn right along a tarmac path just before the next road, cross a road to a fork and take the left-hand path, following cycleway signs to Cardington. Cross a slip road, pass under the A421, cross another slip road and keep ahead along the road into Cardington.

Cardington is a most attractive village with a church, pub - the **Kings Arms** - and old cottages grouped around a green. Although the imposing church looks medieval, it was mostly rebuilt around 1900. The village has strong links with the RAF. Just before reaching the church, and village green, the route continues to the right Ⓑ

along Harrowden Lane. Across the fields to the left the greensand ridge can be seen on the horizon and after $^3/_4$ mile (1.2km), you reach a crossroads. Keep ahead along narrow Old Harrowden Road through Harrowden and in front of the gate to Bunyan Farm, turn right along an enclosed track Ⓒ. After passing under the A421 again, the track bends first left and then right to a road. Cross over, turn right along the track opposite and at a public footpath sign, turn left along a hedge-lined path, heading towards houses on the edge of Bedford.

A short distance before reaching them, turn left beside a barrier Ⓓ and follow the clearly-defined Bunyan Trail across meadows. The path later becomes a tarmac one, keeps beside a stream on the left and finally passes beside a barrier onto a road Ⓔ. Turn right into Elstow, the birthplace of John Bunyan. Despite becoming almost a suburb of Bedford, Elstow is still an attractive village with old timber-framed cottages in the main street and picturesque, early

16th-century Moot Hall. The latter is now a museum of 17th-century English life, with particular reference to Bunyan. Elstow church, in which Bunyan was baptised in 1628, was part of an abbey founded in 1078. It dates from the 12th and 13th centuries and mainly comprises part of the nave and a detached, 15th-century bell tower.

Walk through the village and where the main road bends left, keep ahead along High Street to where the road ends. Continue along a tarmac track to a crossroads and keep ahead along Elstow Road, signposted to Town Centre, for nearly ³/₄ mile (1.2km) to a T-junction **F**. Turn left along St Johns Street and head straight across the roundabout, passing to the left of first St John's Church and then St Mary's Church, to Town Bridge in the centre of Bedford.

Bedford has some handsome public buildings and four fine medieval churches. The most outstanding of these is the majestic St Paul's, seen from the bridge, a large town church of the 14th and 15th centuries, heavily restored in

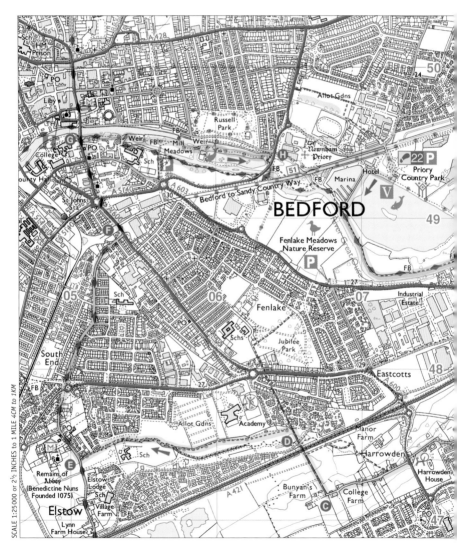

SCALE 1:25000 or 2½ INCHES to 1 MILE 4CM to 1KM

Springtime at Cardington

the Victorian era. The John Bunyan Museum and Free Church stands on the site of the barn where Bunyan preached.

Above all, Bedford is noted for its riverside promenade, along which the next part of the walk proceeds. In front of the bridge, turn right **G** by a hotel onto a tarmac riverside path. Now follow a delightful part of the route as you walk along this tree-lined path by the Great Ouse, crossing two small bridges and bearing right to cross a third one. Follow the path to the left to a T-junction, turn left to cross the weir and then turn right to continue along the tarmac path between two arms of the river – later by a lake on the right.

Just before reaching Newman Bridge and a road, turn right by the end of the lake **H**, passing under a road bridge to a T-junction, and turn right to cross a footbridge over an arm of the river. At a sign for 'Priory Park and Willington', turn left along a tarmac path, recross the river and continue along a tree-lined path.

After crossing another channel of the Great Ouse, keep ahead along a tree-lined track, part of a disused railway line between Bedford and Cambridge and now a footpath and cycleway. Pass beside a barrier, keep ahead to a tarmac drive and turn right into Priory Country Park to return to the start. ●

Woburn Park and Eversholt

		GPS waypoints
Start	Woburn	
Distance	7¼ miles (11.6km)	🥾 SP 949 331
Height gain	460 feet (140m)	**Ⓐ** SP 952 326
Approximate time	3½ hours	**Ⓑ** SP 981 322
Parking	Woburn	**Ⓒ** SP 983 326
Ordnance Survey maps	Explorer 192 (Buckingham & Milton Keynes), Landranger 165 (Aylesbury & Leighton Buzzard)	**Ⓓ** SP 988 338
		Ⓔ SP 981 340
		Ⓕ SP 974 345
		Ⓖ SP 971 334

This is an exceptionally attractive walk and must rank as one of the great classic walks of Bedfordshire. Much of it is across the open expanses of Woburn Deer Park, dotted with trees and lakes. Soon after the start, there is a superb view of Woburn Abbey and near the end, the tower of Woburn Church is seen in the distance across the parkland. The route is well-waymarked and easy-to-follow.

Pevsner describes Woburn as 'a perfect 18th-century village with the character of a small town' and many handsome, brick-built Georgian buildings line the main street. However, the Market House and the church are both Victorian, the latter built in the 1860s by the eighth Duke of Bedford.

🥾 Start in the Market Place by the Market House and walk along George Street, in the Leighton Buzzard direction. After ½ mile (800m), turn left, at a Greensand Ridge Walk sign **Ⓐ**, and go through a kissing-gate by a lodge to enter Woburn Park.

Walk along a fence-lined path and after going through the next kissing-gate, keep ahead across the open expanses of the deer park. The route is clearly marked by a line of short posts and there is a fine view to the right of the façade of Woburn Abbey, the palatial residence of the dukes of Bedford and one of the grandest of England's great houses. The house is built on the site of a medieval abbey whose lands were given to the Russell family, later earls and dukes of Bedford, following the dissolution of the monasteries in the 16th century. The original house was partly destroyed by fire but was restored in the 17th century and then rebuilt in the 18th century. It has a series of sumptuous state rooms and is a treasure house of paintings, furniture and porcelain. The park was landscaped by Humphry Repton in the 18th century.

Pass between two lakes, cross a drive and keep ahead, passing to the left of the house, to join a tarmac drive. Continue along the straight drive, passing beside a barrier, and where it curves right, continue across the deer park, following a line of short posts again. At the far end, negotiate – in quick succession – a wooden gate, iron gate and stile and head gently downhill through a young plantation. Continue through more mature woodland and then across a field. Descend steps, cross a footbridge and keep ahead to cross another footbridge and go through a metal gate. Walk diagonally across a field and continue in the same direction across the next field. On the far side, at a footpath post, the path curves right through an area of rough pasture to emerge, via a gate, onto a road **B**.

Turn left into Eversholt, a widely-scattered village that comprises 13 separate 'ends' or hamlets. Follow the road around several bends, passing the medieval church, opposite which is the **Green Man** pub, and at a left turn, keep ahead along an enclosed tarmac track to the right of a sign, Brook End, **C**. Where it ends, continue along a tree- and hedge-lined path and look out for where you turn left over a plank footbridge. Go through a kissing-gate,

turn right along the edge of a field and go through another kissing-gate. Keep along the right edge of the next field, turn left in the corner, turn right through a kissing-gate and turn left to continue along the enclosed path. This avoids a stretch where the path becomes the bed of a stream. The path heads gently uphill to a gate onto a road.

Cross over, take the track opposite and at a public footpath sign by a farm, turn left **D** – here leaving the Greensand Ridge Walk – and walk diagonally across a field to a kissing-gate. Go through and continue through a young plantation following waymarked signs. Go through a hedge gap and keep along the left edge of the next field and in the corner, bear slightly left through a gap and continue along an enclosed track. Where the track curves right to a farm, turn left, at a

Woburn village

Woburn Abbey

fence corner – the path here may be overgrown – and go through a gate onto a lane. Turn left downhill and after ¼ mile (400m), turn right over a stile **E**, at a public footpath sign, and head gently uphill along an enclosed, grassy path.

The path continues through woodland and after going through a gate, you re-enter Woburn Park. At first continue through woodland and then follow a grassy path across the deer park. The path bends left beside a metal fence to keep along the left edge of Hay Wood and at a footpath post just before reaching a tarmac drive, turn left along a grassy path parallel to the drive **F**. Beyond the high wire fence over to the right is Woburn Safari Park.

Where the drive bears right, keep ahead along a clear grassy path – the

way marked by a line of short posts again – to a road **G**. Cross over, turn right along a grassy path beside it and after about 200 yards, the path bears left away from the road to continue across the park. Keep ahead in a more or less straight line all the time across the rolling parkland, eventually passing the end of Horse Pond to reach the main vehicle drive to Woburn Abbey. Turn right and where the drive bends right, turn left and then almost immediately

right along a tarmac track and go through a gate beside a cattle-grid.

Continue along a track and just before it bends right, bear slightly left along a path which passes along the edge of Upper Drakeloe Pond and continues to a road. Go through a gate by a lodge and turn left to return to the starting point of the walk.

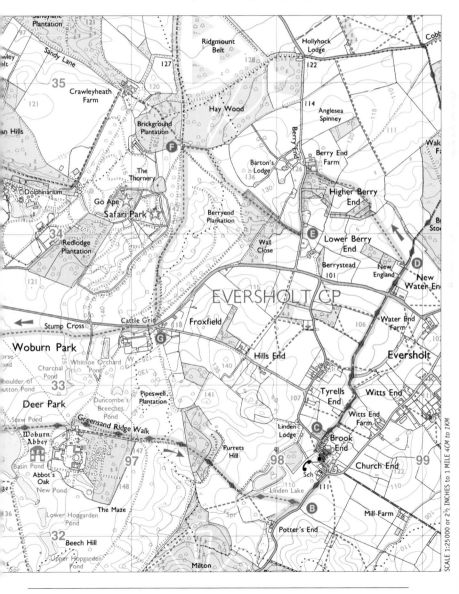

Ampthill Park and Millbrook Warren

		GPS waypoints
Start	Ampthill	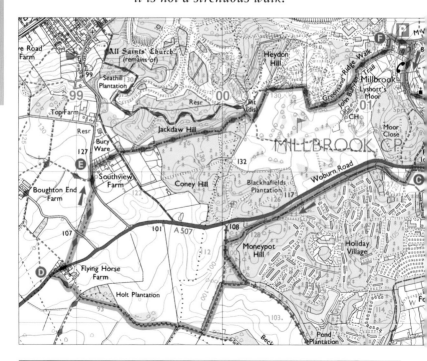 TL 034 382
Distance	8½ miles (13.7km)	Ⓐ TL 032 384
Height gain	735 feet (225m)	Ⓑ TL 016 383
Approximate time	4 hours	Ⓒ TL 013 380
Parking	Ampthill	Ⓓ SP 988 373
Ordnance Survey maps	Explorers 192 (Buckingham & Milton Keynes) and 193 (Luton & Stevenage), Landranger 153 (Bedford & Huntingdon)	Ⓔ SP 991 380
		Ⓕ TL 011 388

An opening ramble along the greensand ridge through Ampthill Park is followed by a walk through the woodlands of Millbrook Common. Then comes an undulating section across fields and through more woodland to the village of Millbrook. Much of this attractive and absorbing route is on the well-waymarked Greensand Ridge Walk and, from the ridge, there are fine and extensive views. Although quite lengthy and with several climbs, it is not a strenuous walk.

Ampthill is basically a Georgian town and a number of attractive 18th-century houses line its main streets, especially Church Street.

✏ Start by walking along Church Street from the road junction in the town centre and at a footpath post opposite Church Avenue, turn left to the mainly 15th-century ironstone church.

Continue along a track to the left of it and at a fork and public footpath sign, take the left-hand track which curves gradually left to a Circular Route post. Bear left to head uphill along a path (Holly Walk) which keeps by the left inside edge of woodland and go through a kissing-gate onto a road. Turn sharp left and at a public footpath sign, turn right Ⓐ and follow the path to the left into Ampthill Park. This was originally the deer park of the now vanished Ampthill Castle and was landscaped by 'Capability' Brown in the 18th century.

Keep in a straight line across the grassland, trees and gorse bushes of the park and at a footpath post, bear slightly left – here joining the Greensand Ridge Walk – to reach a fork by Katherine's Cross. This is on the site of the royal castle and was erected to commemorate Katherine of Aragon, who lived here for several years. At the fork, take the right-hand path, cross a track and continue downhill through trees. Cross another track to a footbridge, cross that, keep ahead across a field towards woodland, climb a stile and follow a path through the trees. Ascend steps to climb a stile, turn left along a winding enclosed path, cross a track and keep ahead to join a track.

At a public footpath sign, turn left Ⓑ – here leaving the Greensand Ridge Walk – along a track to the A507. Turn right, keep ahead at a crossroads and at a waymarked bridleway, turn left Ⓒ and walk along a path towards conifers. After 175 yards, at a crossways and

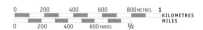

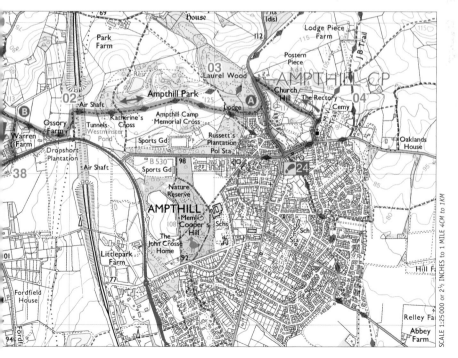

SCALE 1:25 000 or 2½ INCHES to 1 MILE 4CM to 1KM

Katherine's Cross, Ampthill Park

with Woburn Forest Center Parcs ahead, turn right, following the bridlepath that passes around the northern perimeter of the holiday village for almost one mile (1.5km). Reaching the western boundary of the forest, at a T-junction of tracks, swing left and keep to the main byway through woodland to the edge of the trees on the south-western boundary of the forest. Pass into the field and turn right, keeping to the field edge with trees on the right. Follow the field-edge path round a left bend and continue to the left of a line of conifers and cross a track on the edge of the wood. Turn right along a track by the left edge of the trees. Reaching a crossing between fields, go straight over, staying on the right edge of a hedge-lined field. Cross a footbridge and keep to the right-hand field edge to go over another one at the corner of a plantation. Continue across a field towards Flying Horse Farm, going through a gap in the fence and turning left onto the enclosed path. When you reach a gate, pass through to meet the A507 again Ⓓ.

Turn right and at a public footpath sign, turn left and walk diagonally across a field to go through a hedge gap. Turn right along a lane but almost immediately turn left, head uphill along the left edge of a field and go through a hedge gap onto a road. Turn left, at a Greensand Ridge Walk sign turn right Ⓔ along a track, pass to the left of farm buildings and keep ahead to a junction of tracks. Bear right – in the direction of a Greensand Ridge Walk sign – along a track, go through a gate, continue along the drive to Jackdaw Hill House and pass in front of the house to a gate.

Go through and keep ahead through the delightful woodlands of Jackdaw Hill to a T-junction. Turn left and at the next T-junction by the corner of a pond, turn right along a track which bends left and continues along the right inside edge of woodland adjacent to a golf course. The track bends right at a footpath post and soon bends right again to descend steeply. At the bottom, turn left to walk along a broad track. Continue through woodland, then along an enclosed path and bear left to emerge onto a road Ⓕ.

Turn right uphill and take the first road on the right into Millbrook, an estate village formerly belonging to the dukes of Bedford. At a Greensand Ridge Walk sign, turn left, pass beside a barrier and head uphill along an enclosed tarmac path to the medieval church, much restored in the 19th century. Bear right to continue along an enclosed track and, at a footpath sign Ⓑ, you rejoin the outward route and retrace your steps through Ampthill Park to the starting point of the walk.

For a quicker return, on reaching the road Ⓐ turn right downhill back into the centre of Ampthill. ●

Sandy and Everton

		GPS waypoints	
Start	Tourist information centre behind Market Square		TL 173 492
Distance	9 miles (14.5km)	Ⓐ	TL 175 490
Height gain	490 feet (150m)	Ⓑ	TL 183 492
		Ⓒ	TL 194 528
Approximate time	4 hours	Ⓓ	TL 213 524
Parking	Town centre car park at the back of the tourist information centre	Ⓔ	TL 199 509
Ordnance Survey maps	Explorer 208 (Bedford & St Neots), Landranger 153 (Bedford & Huntingdon)		

After an opening stretch through woodland, the route heads across fields at the base of the Greensand Ridge before climbing onto it. Then comes a walk along the ridge, passing through the village of Everton, before descending and retracing steps to the start. From the ridge top – and particularly on the descent – there are extensive views across north Bedfordshire.

Start outside the tourist information centre and walk along High Street, passing to the left of the medieval church, heavily restored in the Victorian era. Turn left into St Swithuns Way Ⓐ and take the first road on the right. Turn left, at a Greensand Ridge Walk sign, along an enclosed tarmac path and cross a footbridge over a railway line.

Go through a kissing-gate, keep ahead across a field towards woodland and at a T-junction just after entering the trees, turn left – not sharp left – along a path that heads up through the attractive woodland of the Pinnacle, curving first left and then right to a fork. Take the right-hand path – follow the regular Greensand Ridge Walk signs as there are lots of paths through the wood – and pass beside a gate onto a lane. Turn right to emerge from the trees and just before reaching a road, turn left through a gate, at public bridleway and Greensand Ridge

Walk signs Ⓑ.

The bridleway follows the route of a Roman road that ran between St Albans and Godmanchester. Walk across a field, bearing left away from the edge, go through a gate and keep ahead across the next field to another gate. Go

Woodland near Sandy

The Greensand Ridge Walk near Everton

edge – to a gate.

Turn left in front of the gate, head uphill along the right edge of a field and in the corner, the path bears right and continues up through trees to join an enclosed track. Keep ahead but look out for where you turn right through a kissing-gate **D**, here rejoining the Greensand Ridge Walk for the rest of the route. Walk across a field, go through a kissing-gate and keep ahead across grass to join a tarmac drive. Follow the drive across Woodbury Park, passing to the left of Woodbury Hall, built in the early 19th century on the site of an earlier house, and continue into the village of Everton.

through, keep ahead first along the right edge of the next two fields and then along an enclosed track and, after passing to the right of barns, the track broadens out. At a fingerpost, keep ahead to a road, cross over and continue along a tarmac path by the right edge of a field. Keep ahead along the right edge of the next field and bear right on joining a wide concrete track. This is part of the disused Tempsford Airfield, built in 1941 and used in the Second World War as a base for Special Operations Executive agents. The barn which is preserved as a memorial to those agents, is on private land.

Where the concrete ends, keep ahead along a straight, wide track and at a fork **C**, take the right-hand track which bends right to another fork. Continue along the left-hand track which bends left along the left edge of a field and at a footpath post, follow the track as it bends right and heads across the field towards the Greensand Ridge. Later the track keeps by the left edge of woodland and at a fingerpost, turns left to continue along the left edge of the next field. At the next fingerpost, it bends right across a field – later along its left

Pass to the right of the mainly Norman church and keep ahead along a lane to a junction by the **Thornton Arms**. Keep ahead along Sandy Road and at a Greensand Ridge Walk sign, turn right along a hedge-lined track **E**. After going through a kissing-gate, head downhill across a field to go through a further two kissing-gates. Follow a track along the right edge of a field to a T-junction. Turn left, here rejoining the outward route, and retrace your steps to the start. ●

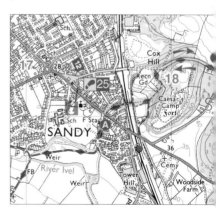

0	200	400	600	800 METRES	1
					KILOMETRES
					MILES
0	200	400	600 YARDS	½	

24

53
Bottom
Farm
26

Hare's
Home

Woodbury
Sinks
34

C

Gibraltar
Farm

Crow
Grove

Woodbury
Home Farm

D

Storymoat
Spinney

Foxhole
Wood

Woodbury Park

Woodbury

Tempsford Road

52

Resr

Woodbury
Hall

White W

EVERTON CP

Victoria
Farm

Story
Moats

Oliver's
Rest

Story
Farm
64

23

Fernbury
Farm

ROMAN ROAD
(course of)

Warden
Hill
54

Park
Farm

Keepers
Lodge

Burford
Farm

Spr

Everton

Sch

51

BP

Euro Const & Co Const B

E

Potton Road

Solitaire

21

Everton Road

Sandy Road

19

68

20

Everton
Park

Sunnymead

Hazells Hall
Farm

Sandy
Heath

50

Mill Lane (Track)

The
Rookery

28

Hasell Hedge

Hazells
Hall

62

Pot
Wind

Long Riding (Track)

ge Walk

Lord's
Wood

64 Everton Road

Potton

Sandy
TV Station

Sand
Pit

Pit
(dis)

Deepdale

Snow
Hill

49

Sandy Road

Cem

DY CP

Sandy Heath

arry
ills

Resr

Woodcock
Covert

B 1042

64

Potton Road

50

37

Fen
Farm

33

Sand & Grave
Pit

66

P

SCALE 1:25000 or 2½ INCHES to 1 MILE 4CM to 1KM

Clophill, Wrest Park and Silsoe

Start	Clophill	
Distance	8¾ miles (14.1km)	
Height gain	545 feet (165m)	
Approximate time	4 hours	
Parking	Roadside parking around The Green at Clophill	
Ordnance Survey maps	Explorer 193 (Luton & Stevenage), Landranger 153 (Bedford & Huntingdon)	

GPS waypoints

- TL 082 376
- Ⓐ TL 083 381
- Ⓑ TL 091 387
- Ⓒ TL 091 381
- Ⓓ TL 096 372
- Ⓔ TL 112 359
- Ⓕ TL 109 359
- Ⓖ TL 082 356
- Ⓗ TL 067 357
- Ⓙ TL 082 374

There is plenty of variety on this lengthy but relatively undemanding and well-waymarked walk. It includes three attractive villages, three churches – one ruined – a 19th-century mansion and a magnificent formal garden. In addition, there is pleasant woodland and a succession of extensive views over Bedfordshire.

A number of 17th- and 18th-century houses line the pleasant village green in Clophill where the walk begins.

Take the tarmac track to the left of the **Green Man** pub, walk through the pub car park, continue along a path to a road and turn right. Turn left at a T-junction, turn right at the next T-junction and where the road bends right after the **Stone Jug** pub, turn left Ⓐ, at a Greensand Ridge Walk post, along a lane (The Slade). Just after the lane becomes a rough track, turn right along a path through trees.

Climb a stile, keep ahead by a fence on the right and go through a kissing-gate. Head up to climb a stile, ascend steps and climb another kissing-gate on the top of the Greensand Ridge. Keep ahead along the right edge of a field, pass through a kissing-gate and turn right along an enclosed track which

passes in front of farm buildings and bends right to a T-junction. Turn left along a lane, at the next T-junction turn right along Great Lane and at a Greensand Ridge Walk sign, turn left through a fence gap. Walk along an enclosed path, in the corner keep ahead through a belt of trees, pass beside a barrier and continue to a T-junction by Clophill Old Church Ⓑ. This ruined medieval hilltop church was replaced by a new church down in the village in the 19th century.

Turn right downhill along an enclosed track to a road on the eastern edge of Clophill, turn right – the new church is ahead – and at a public footpath sign, turn left Ⓒ. Pass beside a barrier, walk along an enclosed path, pass beside another barrier, cross a footbridge over the little River Flit and keep ahead to cross a second footbridge

Gardens at Wrest Park

over another arm of the river. The route ahead is blocked by a large lake, formed as a result of extraction, and the right of way has been diverted. Turn right alongside the river, by a wire fence on the left, and keep beside the fence, following it around two left bends. At the next fence corner, turn right to resume the original route and where the fence bears left, keep ahead across the field to a stile.

Climb it, veer slightly left to head gently uphill across the next field – a line of waymarked posts show the way – and on the far side, climb a stile onto the A507 ⓓ. To the left is the mound of a vanished castle. Cross carefully, take the road opposite (signposted to Gravenhurst) and after nearly ¹/₂ mile (800m), turn left through a hedge gap, at a public footpath sign, and turn right to enter a field. Bear left to head diagonally uphill across the field, go through a hedge gap, continue in the same direction across the next field and go through a hedge gap onto a track. Turn left, at a public footpath sign turn right to walk across a field, later

continuing along the right edge of the next field and go through a kissing-gate in the corner.

Continue along the right edge of the next field, go through a kissing-gate, keep ahead to a T-junction and turn left along an enclosed path. The path turns right and at the next T-junction, turn right and keep ahead into the churchyard at Upper Gravenhurst. Pass to the right of the medieval church and go through a gap onto a road ⓔ. The route continues to the right to a T-junction.

Turn right uphill and at a public bridleway sign, turn left along a track ⓕ. This straight track initially runs along a broad ridge, with superb views all around, and later gently descends to Wrest Park. At a public bridleway sign, it becomes a tarmac drive which continues between the buildings of Silsoe Research Institute and passes to the right of Wrest Park House and Gardens. There is very much a French theme at Wrest Park. The fine gardens, created by Henry de Grey, first Duke of Kent, in the first half of the 18th century, were heavily influenced by

SCALE 1:25000 or 2½ INCHES to 1 MILE 4CM to 1KM

```
0    200   400   600   800 METRES   1
                                    KILOMETRES
                                    MILES
0    200   400   600 YARDS   ½
```

those at Versailles and the house was built between 1834 and 1839 in the style of a French chateau.

Keep ahead along the drive to cross a bridge over the A6 and continue into Silsoe, passing to the right of the 19th-century church. At a crossroads **G** keep ahead, bear right at a T-junction and continue along Holly Walk. Where the road ends at a public footpath sign, go through a gate and continue along a track, passing to the right of Silsoe Horticultural Centre. At a crossways, keep ahead along a path which eventually emerges onto a road at Wardhedges and turn right **H**. *For the* **Jolly Coopers** *pub turn left, and then bear right along Wardhedges Road.*

At both public footpath and bridleway signs, leave the lane and in 50 yards turn left at a public footpath

sign through a gap in the hedge on the left just past a white gate. Continue on a field-edge path that curves gradually right to a road. Cross over, pass beside the gate opposite and keep ahead along a track. At a fork, take the right-hand track –it keeps first along the left edge of a field, then it becomes enclosed, then continues along a right field edge – which eventually curves left to a waymarked post in the field corner.

Keep ahead through a hedge gap and walk along a track which keeps by the left inside edge of the superb woodland of Simpsonhill Plantation to emerge through a gate onto the A6 **J**. Turn left, almost immediately turn right to cross carefully this busy road and walk along Old Silsoe Road. Take the first road on the left and where it ends, cross the A507 by a footbridge. Keep ahead to cross a footbridge over the River Flit to return to The Green in Clophill.

The Ayots, Brocket Park and the River Lea

		GPS waypoints
Start	Wheathampstead	📝 TL 177 140
Distance	10 miles (16.2km)	Ⓐ TL 185 141
Height gain	675 feet (205m)	Ⓑ TL 181 160
Approximate time	5 hours	Ⓒ TL 192 168
Parking	Wheathampstead	Ⓓ TL 202 153
Ordnance Survey maps	Explorer 182 (St Albans & Hatfield), Landranger 166 (Luton & Hertford)	Ⓔ TL 210 143
		Ⓕ TL 221 140
		Ⓖ TL 216 129
		Ⓗ TL 203 138

Although this is a lengthy walk, the terrain is undemanding and the paths are generally clear and well-waymarked. The Ayots are a group of three villages between Wheathampstead and Welwyn Garden City and the route goes through two of them. There are pleasant opening and closing stretches beside the River Lea, fine views, attractive woodland and a particularly memorable ramble through Brocket Park. The walk also passes the former home of George Bernard Shaw.

📝 The walk begins by the large, mainly 13th-century, cruciform church. With your back to it, turn left down High Street and just after crossing the bridge over the River Lea, turn right, at a public bridleway sign to Waterend, along a paved path. Continue along a road through a housing estate and where it ends, go through a gap beside a gate and keep ahead along a partially tree-lined track which narrows to a path.

Go through a gate, walk along the right edge of a field, go through a gate in the corner and turn right along a fence-lined path. Go through another gate onto a track Ⓐ, turn left, go under a road bridge and, after passing beside a gate, continue gently uphill along a tree-lined track. After about 50 yards, turn left up a path, go through a gate, walk across a field, go through another

gate and descend to cross a track. Head up to climb a stile and walk along an enclosed path to emerge onto a lane by the entrance to Lamerwood Country Club.

Go through a kissing-gate to the left of the entrance, walk along a grassy path which runs parallel to a tarmac track on the right and at a waymarked post, continue along the track. At a fork, take the right-hand track to a footpath post at a junction of tracks, turn left and head across to a waymarked post on the edge of woodland. Continue along the right inside edge of the trees, go through a gate and turn right along a track – it later becomes a tarmac one – to a three-way fork in front of the gates of Lamer Park Farm Ⓑ.

Bear right to climb a stile and continue along a straight, fence- and tree-lined path, Climb a stile, keep ahead and the path curves slightly left to a crossways. Turn right onto a path by the left inside edge of woodland and at a waymarked post, turn left up steps. Walk along the right edge of this field and pass beside a gate to join a lane. Turn right and where the lane bears right, keep ahead through a kissing-gate, at a public footpath sign, and walk across two fields, going through a series of kissing-gates and finally keeping ahead along a track to a lane in Ayot St Lawrence . The **Brocket Arms** pub and the ruined, mainly 13th-century, church are to the left. When a new Grecian-style church was built in the 18th century, the old one became redundant and was used as a source of building material.

The route continues to the right to Shaw's Corner. The modest Edwardian villa here was the home of George Bernard Shaw from 1906 until his death in 1950 and remains much as he left it. Keep ahead, in the Wheathampstead

Ruined church at Ayot St Lawrence

direction, follow the lane around a left bend and where it bends right, keep ahead, at a public bridleway sign, along an enclosed path. Follow the path – sometimes through woodland and sometimes with views over open country – to a road , cross over to a public bridleway sign and continue along a path which follows the curving edge of the trees on the left. Pass beside a gate, keep initially along the right edge of woodland and the path later continues through the trees. On emerging from them, walk along the left edge of a field and after passing through a hedge gap, continue along the right edge of the next field towards a disused railway bridge.

In front of the bridge , turn right up to a track and turn left to cross the bridge. This former railway track is now the Ayot Greenway, a footpath and cycleway between Wheathampstead and Welwyn Garden City. Keep along the track for nearly ¹⁄₂ mile (800m) until you reach the second set of stiles and climb the stile on the right. Turn sharp right along the right edge of a field and when you are parallel to the corner of woodland across the field to the left, turn left, head across to the corner of the wood and take the path that descends by the right inside edge of the trees to a stile.

Climb it, walk along a hedge-lined path, climb another stile, continue gently uphill along a narrow enclosed path and go through a fence gap onto a lane. Turn left, keep ahead at a junction and at a T-junction, turn left and follow the lane through the pretty village of Ayot Green. Just before reaching the bridge over the A1(M), turn right along Brickwall Close and at a public footpath sign opposite the **Waggoners** pub, turn right through a kissing-gate and walk along an enclosed path to enter Brocket Park.

After passing through a fence gap, continue through woodland and across a golf course – the route clearly indicated by regular waymarked posts – eventually to join a tarmac drive.

Immediately turn sharp right **G** along a path by the left edge of the golf course – here joining the Lea Valley Walk for the rest of the way. Cross a drive and turn left beside a fence on the left. From

here is a fine view of Brocket Hall, an elegant Georgian mansion and the home of two of Queen Victoria's prime ministers, Lord Melbourne and Lord Palmerston. It is now a conference centre.

Keep in a straight line and at the corner of the fence, continue across the golf course to enter woodland. Follow a path through the wood and after steeply descending a wooded ridge, continue along an enclosed path which emerges onto a lane at Waterend. Turn right by Waterend House on the right (built in 1610) and at a public footpath sign 'Lea Valley Walk, Wheathampstead', turn left along an enclosed path . Follow the regular Lea Valley Walk signs, later keeping along the left edge of fields, to a kissing-gate. Go through, continue across a riverside meadow and at a fork, take the left-hand path to go through another kissing-gate.

Keep along the left field edge, continue across the field corner to climb a stile on the far side and turn right along a narrow fence-lined path which curves left. Descend steps to a track and turn left under a road bridge A. Here you pick up the outward route and retrace your steps to the start.

St Albans and the Ver valley

St Albans and the Ver valley

		GPS waypoints
Start	St Albans, Market Place	TL 147 072
Distance	10½ miles (16.8km)	**A** TL 142 068
Height gain	495 feet (150m)	**B** TL 135 074
Approximate time	5 hours	**C** TL 137 079
Parking	St Albans,	**D** TL 142 109
Ordnance Survey maps	Explorer 182 (St Albans & Hatfield), Landranger 166 (Luton & Hertford)	**E** TL 145 116
		F TL 138 119
		G TL 120 108
		H TL 125 089
		J TL 126 032

Although a long walk, the gradients are gentle and route finding is relatively easy. A walk through Verulamium Park, site of a Roman city, is followed by a lengthy but easy ascent to the hamlet of Childwick Green and on to the edge of Harpenden Common. Then comes a descent back into the Ver valley to Redbournbury Mill and a walk beside the little river through the Gorhambury Estate, using a combination of public rights of way and permissive paths. There are fine views across the valley and leave plenty of time for an exploration of St Albans, a particularly attractive and interesting city.

Note that the permissive paths between points **H** and **B** on the return leg of the walk may be closed on certain days. In that case, the alternative route along roads, shown on the map, would have to be used.

Unlike most towns of Roman origin in England, St Albans grew up on a different site from the Roman settlement. The medieval town developed around the abbey that was founded in 793 on the spot where Alban, the first British Christian martyr, was executed in the early 3rd century. During the Middle Ages, the abbey became one of the wealthiest in the country, its coffers swelled by the numerous pilgrims who visited the shrine of St Alban. After Henry VIII's dissolution of the monasteries in the

1530s, it became a parish church and when a new diocese was created in 1877, it provided a ready-made cathedral.

Despite many changes and rebuildings, St Albans Cathedral is still basically the Norman abbey that was begun in the late 11th century. It is one of the longest churches in the country and bricks from the Roman city of Verulamium were used in its construction, their red tints apparent especially in the fine central tower. Internally, the cathedral is a mixture of

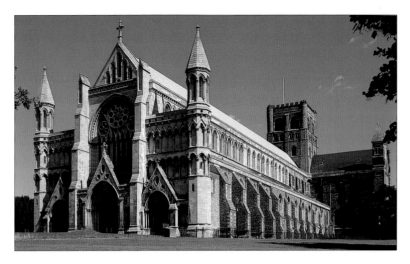
St Albans Cathedral

the Norman and Gothic styles and is noted for possessing some of the finest surviving early wall paintings in the country. In Victorian times, the poor condition of the building necessitated a major restoration.

The walk begins in the Market Place. Facing the former town hall (now tourist information centre), walk along the street to the right of it and, at a fork, take the right-hand street (French Row) to a T-junction by the 15th-century clock tower. Cross over, go under the arch straight ahead and follow a paved path to the cathedral. After the path curves left, bear right past the east end of the cathedral to a T-junction and turn right along the south side of the cathedral.

The path bends first left and then right and at a fork, take the left-hand tarmac path which heads gently downhill across grass.

At the bottom, bear right **A**, pass to the left of the **Fighting Cocks** pub, turn left to cross a bridge over the River Ver and turn right to continue along a tarmac path across Verulamium Park, between the lake on the left and the river on the right. Most of Verulamium, one of the major cities of Roman Britain, lies under the park, but fragments of the walls can be seen on the other side of the lake. There are other stretches of the walls and the foundations of one of the gates, a hypocaust and the remains of a theatre are visible above ground. There is also a superb museum, situated near St Michael's Church.

Beyond the end of the lake, the path emerges onto a road. Turn left and the road bends right by St Michael's Church to a main road (A4147) **B**. Turn right, at a crossroads keep ahead along Batchwood Drive and at a public bridleway sign, turn left along a tarmac track **C**. Follow this winding track for $^1/_2$ mile (800m) – there is a golf course on the right – and about 100 yards after a right bend, look out for where a waymarked post directs you to turn left along a tree-lined path. The path curves right gently uphill, keeps along the right edge of a field and at a hedge corner, continues across the field towards trees. On the far side, keep ahead along an enclosed path, by the right edge of Ladies Grove Wood, to emerge onto a tarmac track.

As you walk along it, fine views open up to the left over the Ver valley. After

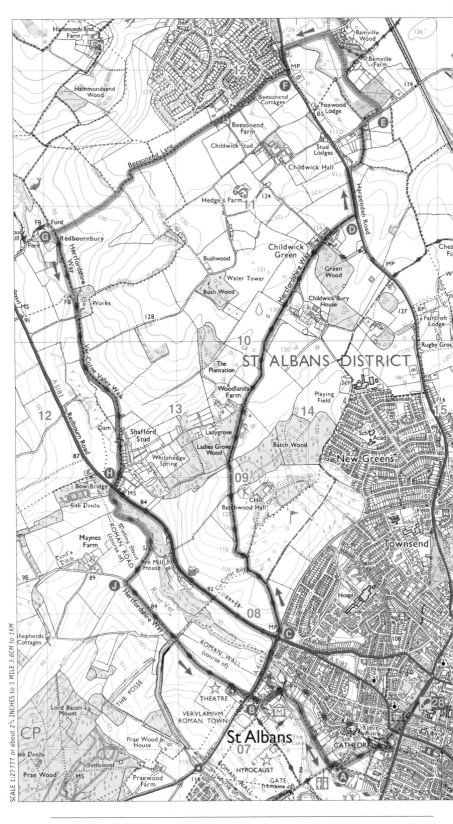

St Albans

passing to the left of a large house (Childwick Bury), continue along a wider track, go through a gate and keep ahead into the pleasant estate hamlet of Childwick Green. Pass the small, redbrick Victorian church and continue to the A1081 **D**. Turn left and at a public footpath sign, turn right and descend an embankment to a kissing-gate. Go through, turn left along the left edge of a field, climb a stile, continue along a pleasantly tree-lined path and climb a stile onto a lane.

Turn right, take the first lane on the left **E** (East Common) and follow it across part of Harpenden Common, passing the **Three Horseshoes** pub. At a crossroads, turn left along a lane (Cross Lane) to return to the A1081, turn left and take the first lane on the right (Beesonend Lane) **F**. Take the left-hand lane at a fork – there is a No Through Road sign – and keep along this narrow lane for nearly 1 1/2 miles (2.4km), descending gently into the valley. Where the lane bends right in front of a farm and becomes a rough track, the route continues to the left **G**, joining

the Ver Valley Walk, but it is worthwhile making a short detour to Redbournbury Mill.

For this detour, follow the track to the right, cross a footbridge over the Ver, walk along a track, cross another footbridge and keep ahead to the mill. Now a museum and regularly open to the public, there has possibly been a mill on this site since Norman times.

Retrace your steps to where you joined the Ver Valley Walk **G** and keep ahead along the track, by trees on the right, to a kissing-gate. Go through, walk along the left edge of a meadow, go through another kissing-gate at the far, tapering end and continue through a belt of trees. Keep ahead across grass, cross a tarmac track, go through a kissing-gate and follow a path beside the river to join a tarmac track.

Continue along the path, going through a gate by a farm, to emerge onto the A5183 **H**. Cross over and go through the gate opposite. From here to point **B** the route is along permissive paths across the Gorhambury Estate. Walk along a well-waymarked path across meadows and through trees, following the curves of the Ver, and after crossing a footbridge, turn right to cross the river and continue along a tarmac track to a T-junction **J**. Turn left along a straight, tree-lined, tarmac track – ahead is a fine view of St Albans Cathedral – and go through a gate to the left of the Roman theatre, built in the 2nd century AD and one of only six believed to have existed in Britain.

Keep ahead to the A4147 **B**. After crossing it, you pick up the outward route and retrace your steps through the park to the start.

| 0 | 200 | 400 | 600 | 800 METRES | 1 | |
| 0 | 200 | 400 | 600 YARDS | 1/2 | | KILOMETRES MILES |

Further Information

The National Trust

Anyone who likes visiting places of natural beauty and/or historic interest has cause to be grateful to the National Trust. Without it, many such places would probably have vanished by now.

It was in response to the pressures on the countryside posed by the relentless march of Victorian industrialisation that the trust was set up in 1895. Its founders, inspired by the common goals of protecting and conserving Britain's national heritage and widening public access to it, were Sir Robert Hunter, Octavia Hill and Canon Rawnsley: respectively a solicitor, a social reformer and a clergyman. The latter was particularly influential. As a canon of Carlisle Cathedral and vicar of Crosthwaite (near Keswick), he was concerned about threats to the Lake District and had already been active in protecting footpaths and promoting public access to open countryside. After the flooding of Thirlmere in 1879 to create a large reservoir, he became increasingly convinced that the only effective way to guarantee protection was outright ownership of land.

The purpose of the National Trust is to preserve areas of natural beauty and sites of historic interest by acquisition, holding them in trust for the nation and making them available for public access and enjoyment. Some of its properties have been acquired through purchase, but many have been donated. Nowadays it is not only one of the biggest landowners in the country, but also one of the most active conservation charities, protecting 581,113 acres (253,176 ha) of land, including 555 miles (892km) of coastline, and more than 300 historic properties in England, Wales and Northern Ireland. (There is a separate National Trust for Scotland, which was set up in 1931.)

Furthermore, once a piece of land has come under National Trust ownership, it is difficult for its status to be altered. As a result of parliamentary legislation in 1907, the Trust was given the right to declare its property inalienable, so ensuring that in any subsequent dispute it can appeal directly to parliament.

As it works towards its dual aims of conserving areas of attractive countryside and encouraging greater public access (not easy to reconcile in this age of mass tourism), the Trust provides an excellent service for walkers by creating new concessionary paths and waymarked trails, maintaining stiles and footbridges and combating the ever-increasing problem of footpath erosion.

For details of membership, contact the National Trust at the address on page 95.

The Ramblers

No organisation works more actively to protect and extend the rights and interests of walkers in the countryside than the Ramblers. Its aims are clear: to foster a greater knowledge, love and care of the countryside; to assist in the protection and enhancement of public rights of way and areas of natural beauty; to work for greater public access to the countryside; and to encourage more people to take up rambling as a healthy, recreational leisure activity.

It was founded in 1935 when, following the setting up of a National Council of Ramblers' Federation in 1931, a number of federations in London, Manchester, the Midlands and elsewhere came together to create a more effective pressure group, to deal with such problems as the disappearance or obstruction of footpaths, the prevention of access to open mountain and moorland, and increasing hostility from landowners. This was the era of the mass trespasses, when there were sometimes violent confrontations between ramblers and gamekeepers, especially on the moorlands of the Peak District.

Dunstable Downs

Since then the Ramblers has played a key role in preserving and developing the national footpath network, supporting the creation of national parks and encouraging the designation and waymarking of long-distance routes.

Our freedom of access to the country-side, now enshrined in legislation, is still in its early years and requires constant vigilance. But over and above this there will always be the problem of footpaths being illegally obstructed, disappearing through lack of use, or being extinguished by housing or road construction.

It is to meet such problems and dangers that the Ramblers exists and represents the interests of all walkers. The address to write to for information on the Ramblers and how to become a member is given on page 95.

 ## Walkers and the Law

The *Countryside and Rights of Way Act 2000 (CRoW)* gives a public right of access in England and Wales to land mapped as open country (mountain, moor, heath and down) or registered common land. These areas are known as *open access land*, and include land around the coastline, known as *coastal margin*.

Where You Can Go
Rights of Way
Prior to the introduction of *CRoW* walkers could only legally access the countryside along public rights of way. These are either 'footpaths' (for walkers only) or 'bridleways' (for walkers, riders on horseback and pedal cyclists). A third category called 'Byways open to all traffic' (BOATs), is used by motorised vehicles as well as those using non-mechanised transport. Mainly they are green lanes, farm and estate roads, although occasionally they will be found crossing mountainous area.

Rights of way are marked on Ordnance Survey maps. Look for the green broken lines on the Explorer maps, or the red dashed lines on Landranger maps.

The term 'right of way' means exactly what it says. It gives a right of passage over what, for the most part, is private land. Under pre-CRoW legislation walkers were required to keep to the line of the right of way and not stray onto land on either side. If you did inadvertently wander off the right of way, either because of faulty map reading or because the route was not clearly indicated on the ground, you were technically trespassing.

Local authorities have a legal obligation to ensure that rights of way are kept clear and free of obstruction, and are signposted where they leave metalled roads. The duty of local authorities to install signposts extends to the placing of signs along a path or way, but only where the authority considers it necessary to have a signpost or waymark to assist persons unfamiliar with the locality.

CRoW Access Rights
Access Land

As well as being able to walk on existing rights of way, under CRoW legislation you have access to large areas of open land and, under further legislation, a right of coastal access, which is being implemented by Natural England, giving for the first time the right of access around all England's open coast. This includes plans for an England Coast Path (ECP) which will run for 2,795 miles (4,500 kilometres). A corresponding Wales Coast Path has been open since 2012.

Coastal access rights apply within the coastal margin (including along the ECP) unless the land falls into a category of excepted land or is subject to local restrictions, exclusions or diversions.

You can of course continue to use rights of way to cross access land, but you can lawfully leave the path and wander at will in these designated areas.

Where to Walk

Access Land is shown on Ordnance Survey Explorer maps by a light yellow tint surrounded by a pale orange border. New orange coloured 'i' symbols on the maps will show the location of permanent access information boards installed by the access authorities. Coastal Margin is shown on Ordnance Survey Explorer maps by a pink tint.

Restrictions

The right to walk on access land may lawfully be restricted by landowners. Landowners can, for any reason, restrict access for up to 28 days in any year.

They cannot however close the land:
- on bank holidays;
- for more than four Saturdays and Sundays in a year;
- on any Saturday from 1 June to 11 August; or
- on any Sunday from 1 June to the end of September.

They have to provide local authorities with five working days' notice before the date of closure unless the land involved is an area of less than five hectares or the closure is for less than four hours. In these cases landowners only need to provide two hours' notice.

Whatever restrictions are put into place on access land they have no effect on existing rights of way, and you can continue to walk on them.

Dogs

Dogs can be taken on access land, but must be kept on leads of two metres or less between 1 March and 31 July, and at all times where they are near livestock. In addition landowners may impose a ban on all dogs from fields where lambing takes place for up to six weeks in any year. Dogs may be banned from moorland used for grouse shooting and breeding for up to five years.

In the main, walkers following the routes in this book will continue to follow existing rights of way, but a knowledge and understanding of the law as it affects walkers, plus the ability to distinguish access land marked on the maps, will enable anyone who wishes to depart from paths that cross access land either to take a shortcut, to enjoy a view or to explore.

General Obstructions

Obstructions can sometimes cause a problem on a walk and the most common of these is where the path across a field has been ploughed over. It is legal for a farmer to plough up a path provided that it is restored within two weeks. This does not always happen and you are faced with the dilemma of following the line of the path, even if this means treading on crops, or walking round the edge of the field.

Further Information

Countryside Access Charter

Your rights of way are:

- public footpaths – on foot only. Sometimes waymarked in yellow
- bridleways – on foot, horseback and pedal cycle. Sometimes waymarked in blue
- byways (usually old roads), most 'roads used as public paths' and, of course, public roads – all traffic has the right of way

Use maps, signs and waymarks to check rights of way. Ordnance Survey Explorer and Landranger maps show most public rights of way

On rights-of-way you can:

- take a pram, pushchair or wheelchair if practicable
- take a dog (on a lead or under close control)
- take a short route round an illegal obstruction or remove it sufficiently to get past

You have a right to go for recreation to:

- public parks and open spaces – on foot
- most commons near older towns and cities – on foot and sometimes on horseback
- private land where the owner has a formal agreement with the local authority

In addition you can use the following by local or established custom or consent, but ask for advice if you are unsure:

- many areas of open country, such as moorland, fell and coastal areas, especially those in the care of the National Trust, and some commons
- some woods and forests, especially those owned by the Forestry Commission
- country parks and picnic sites
- most beaches
- canal towpaths
- some private paths and tracks Consent sometimes extends to horse-riding and cycling

For your information:

- county councils and London boroughs maintain and record rights-of-way, and register commons
- obstructions, dangerous animals, harassment and misleading signs on rights-of-way are illegal and you should report them to the county council
- paths across fields can be ploughed, but must normally be reinstated within two weeks
- landowners can require you to leave land to which you have no right of access
- motor vehicles are normally permitted only on roads, byways and some 'roads used as public paths'

Further Information

Although the later course of action seems the most sensible, it does mean that you would be trespassing.

Other obstructions can vary from overhanging vegetation to wire fences across the path, locked gates or even a cattle feeder on the path.

Use common sense. If you can get round the obstruction without causing damage, do so. Otherwise only remove as much of the obstruction as is necessary to secure passage.

If the right of way is blocked and cannot be followed, there is a long-standing view that in such circumstances there is a right to deviate, but this cannot wholly be relied on. Although it is accepted in law that highways (and that

includes rights of way) are for the public service, and if the usual track is impassable, it is for the general good that people should be entitled to pass into another line. However, this should not be taken as indicating a right to deviate whenever a way becomes impassable. If in doubt, retreat.

Report obstructions to the local authority and/or the Ramblers.

Global Positioning System (GPS)

What is GPS?

GPS is a worldwide radio navigation system that uses a network of 24 satellites and receivers, usually hand-held, to calculate positions. By measuring the time it takes a signal to reach the receiver, the distance from the satellite can be estimated. Repeat this with several satellites and the receiver can then use triangulation to establish the position of the receiver.

How to use GPS with Ordnance Survey mapping

Each of the walks in this book includes GPS co-ordinate data that reflects the walk position points on Ordnance Survey maps.

GPS and OS maps use different models for the earth and co-ordinate systems, so when you are trying to relate your GPS position to features on the map the two will differ slightly. This is especially the case with height, as the model that relates the GPS global co-ordinate system to height above sea level is very poor.

When using GPS with OS mapping, some distortion – up to 16 feet (5m) – will always be present. Moreover, individual features on maps may have been surveyed only to an accuracy of 23 feet (7m) (for 1:25000 scale maps), while other features, e.g. boulders, are usually only shown schematically.

In practice, this should not cause undue difficulty, as you will be near enough to your objective to be able to spot it.

How to use the GPS data in this book

There are various ways you can use the GPS data in this book.

1. Follow the route description while checking your position on your receiver when you are approaching a position point.

2. You can also use the positioning information on your receiver to verify where you are on the map.

3. Alternatively, you can use some of the proprietary software that is available. At the simple end there is inexpensive software, which lets you input the walk positions (waypoints), download them to the gps unit and then use them to assist your navigation on the walks.

At the upper end of the market Ordnance Survey maps are available in electronic

form. Most come with software that enables you to enter your walking route onto the map, download it to your gps unit and use it, alongside the route description, to follow the route.

 ## *Walking Safety*

Although the reasonably gentle countryside that is the subject of this book offers no real dangers to walkers at any time of the year, it is still advisable to take sensible precautions and follow certain well-tried guidelines.

Always take with you both warm and waterproof clothing and sufficient food and drink. Wear suitable footwear, such as strong walking boots or shoes that give a good grip over stony ground, on slippery slopes and in muddy conditions. Try to obtain a local weather forecast and bear it in mind before you start. Do not be afraid to abandon your proposed route and return to your starting point in the event of a sudden and unexpected deterioration in the weather.

All the walks described in this book will be safe to do, given due care and respect, even during the winter. Indeed, a crisp, fine winter day often provides perfect walking conditions, with firm ground underfoot and a clarity unique to this time of the year. The most difficult hazard likely to be encountered is mud, especially when walking along woodland and field paths, farm tracks and bridleways – the latter in particular can often get churned up by cyclists and horses. In summer, an additional difficulty may be narrow and overgrown paths, particularly along the edges of cultivated fields. Neither should constitute a major problem provided that the appropriate footwear is worn.

 ## *Useful Organisations*

Bedfordshire County Council,
Rights of Way, County Hall,
Cauldwell Street, Bedford MK42 9AP

Tel. 01234 267422
www.bedfordshire.gov.uk

Hertfordshire County Council,
Planning and Environment, County Hall,
Pegs Lane, Hertford SG13 8DQ
Tel. 0300 123 4047
www.hertfordshire.gov.uk

Campaign to Protect Rural England
5-11 Lavington Street,
London SE1 0NZ
Tel. 0207 981 2800
www.cpre.org.uk

Forestry Commission
*South East and London
Area Office*
Bucks Horn Oak, Farnham,
Surrey GU10 4LS
Tel. 0300 067 4420
www.forestry.gov.uk

Long Distance Walkers' Association
www.ldwa.org.uk

National Trust
Membership and general enquiries:
Tel. 0344 800 1895
Regional Office:
London and South East
Email:
lse.customerenquiries@nationaltrust.org.uk
www.nationaltrust.org.uk

Natural England
*Essex, Herts, Beds, Cambs and
Northants Regional Office*
Eastbrook, Shaftesbury Road,
Cambridge CB2 8DR
Tel. 0300 060 1114
www.gov.uk/government/organisations/
natural-england

Ordnance Survey
Tel. 03456 05 05 05 (Lo-call)
www.ordnancesurvey.co.uk

Ramblers
2nd Floor, Camelford House,
87–90 Albert Embankment,
London SE1 7TW.

Tel. 0207 339 8500
www.ramblers.org.uk

Tourist information
Experience Bedfordshire
www.experiencebedfordshire.co.uk
Visit Hertfordshire
www.visitherts.co.uk
Local tourist information centres:
Bedford: 01234 718112
Dunstable: 01582 891420
Hertford: 01992 584322
Letchworth: 01462 530360
St Albans: 01727 864511
Sandy: 01767 682728

Youth Hostels Association,
Trevelyan House,
Dimple Road,
Matlock, Derbyshire
DE4 3YH.
Tel. 01629 592700
www.yha.org.uk.

■ *Ordnance Survey maps of
Hertfordshire and Bedfordshire*
The area of Hertfordshire and Bedfordshire
is covered by Ordnance Survey 1:50 000
($1\frac{1}{4}$ inches to 1 mile or 2cm to 1km) scale
Landranger map sheets 153, 154, 165,
166, 176. These all-purpose maps are
packed with information to help you
explore the area and show viewpoints,
picnic sites, places of interest and caravan
and camping sites.

To examine Hertfordshire and
Bedfordshire in more detail and especially if
you are planning walks, Ordnance Survey
Explorer maps at 1:25 000 ($2\frac{1}{2}$ inches to
1 mile or 4cm to 1km) scale are ideal:

172 Chiltern Hills East
181 Chiltern Hills North
182 St Albans & Hatfield
192 Buckingham & Milton Keynes
193 Luton & Stevenage
194 Hertford & Bishop's Stortford
208 Bedford & St Neots

Ordnance Survey

Pathfinder® Guides 🪧 **Britain's best-loved walking guides**

Scotland
Pathfinder Walks
3 ISLE OF SKYE
4 CAIRNGORMS
7 FORT WILLIAM & GLEN COE
19 DUMFRIES & GALLOWAY
23 LOCH LOMOND, THE TROSSACHS, & STIRLING
27 PERTHSHIRE, ANGUS & FIFE
30 LOCH NESS & INVERNESS
31 OBAN, MULL & KINTYRE
46 ABERDEEN & ROYAL DEESIDE
47 EDINBURGH, PENTLANDS & LOTHIANS

North of England
Pathfinder Walks
15 YORKSHIRE DALES
22 MORE LAKE DISTRICT
28 NORTH YORK MOORS
35 NORTHUMBERLAND & SCOTTISH BORDERS
39 DURHAM, NORTH PENNINES & TYNE AND WEAR
42 CHESHIRE
49 VALE OF YORK & YORKSHIRE WOLDS
53 LANCASHIRE
60 LAKE DISTRICT
63 PEAK DISTRICT
64 SOUTH PENNINES
71 THE HIGH FELLS OF LAKELAND
73 MORE PEAK DISTRICT
Short Walks
1 YORKSHIRE DALES
2 PEAK DISTRICT
3 LAKE DISTRICT
13 NORTH YORK MOORS

Wales
Pathfinder Walks
10 SNOWDONIA
18 BRECON BEACONS
32 NORTH WALES & SNOWDONIA
34 PEMBROKESHIRE & CARMARTHENSHIRE
41 MID WALES
55 GOWER, SWANSEA & CARDIFF
Short Walks
14 SNOWDONIA
31 BRECON BEACONS

Heart of England
Pathfinder Walks
6 COTSWOLDS
14 SHROPSHIRE & STAFFORDSHIRE
20 SHERWOOD FOREST & THE EAST MIDLANDS
29 WYE VALLEY & FOREST OF DEAN
74 THE MALVERNS TO WARWICKSHIRE

Short Walks
4 COTSWOLDS
32 HEREFORDSHIRE & THE WYE VALLEY

East of England
Pathfinder Walks
44 ESSEX
45 NORFOLK
48 SUFFOLK
50 LINCOLNSHIRE & THE WOLDS
51 CAMBRIDGESHIRE & THE FENS

South West of England
Pathfinder Walks
1 SOUTH DEVON & DARTMOOR
5 CORNWALL
9 EXMOOR & THE QUANTOCKS
11 DORSET & THE JURASSIC COAST
21 SOMERSET, THE MENDIPS & WILTSHIRE
26 DARTMOOR
68 NORTH & MID DEVON
69 SOUTH WEST ENGLAND'S COAST
Short Walks
8 DARTMOOR
9 CORNWALL
21 EXMOOR
29 SOUTH DEVON

South East of England
Pathfinder Walks
8 KENT
12 NEW FOREST, HAMPSHIRE & SOUTH DOWNS
25 THAMES VALLEY & CHILTERNS
54 HERTFORDSHIRE & BEDFORDSHIRE
65 SURREY
66 SOUTH DOWNS NATIONAL PARK & WEST SUSSEX
67 SOUTH DOWNS NATIONAL PARK & EAST SUSSEX
72 THE HOME COUNTIES FROM LONDON BY TRAIN
Short Walks
23 NEW FOREST NATIONAL PARK
27 ISLE OF WIGHT

Practical Guide
75 NAVIGATION SKILLS FOR WALKERS

City Walks
LONDON
OXFORD
EDINBURGH